I highly recommend this volume to anyone who wants to know how the United Nations really works. Nowhere else could one find so much wisdom about the world body packed into so few pages. From his unparalleled experience Ambassador Rosenthal draws invaluable lessons for diplomats, policymakers, scholars, and representatives of civil society.

Edward C. Luck, Professor of Professional Practice, Columbia University and former Special Adviser and Assistant Secretary-General, the United Nations

This admirably slim, deeply wise volume from one of Latin America's leading social scientists assesses unsentimentally and in-depth a set of important negotiations in which he was involved at the United Nations, generally in a leading role, over nearly two decades. The narrative achieves a deep dive into intra-UN dynamics

David Malone, Rector of the United Nations University and Under-Secretary-General of the United Nations

Gert Rosenthal has written a fascinating and important book. Very few people can have seen this hidden landscape from as many different perches as Ambassador Rosenthal. This text will be an indispensable primer for diplomats and policy makers at the UN as much as for students and scholars of multilateral diplomacy.

Sarah F. Cliffe, Director, Center on International Cooperation, New York University

Inside the United Nations

This book illustrates the parameters surrounding consensus-building at the United Nations, seeking to provide new insights beyond what is already known. The author spent twelve years as P.R. of Guatemala at the UN, offering him privileged observatories in all three of the main inter-governmental organs: the General Assembly, the Economic and Social Council, and the Security Council. In this book Rosenthal focuses on six case studies that offer the breadth and scope of what the UN does, and illustrate some of the main elements of the dynamics of consensus-building, providing concrete examples of the ingredients that shape decision-making in a multilateral setting. The chapters:

- cover the origin and preparation and outcome of two successful international conferences: the 2000 Millennium Summit and the 2002 International Conference on Financing for Development;
- look at the 2000 negotiation on the scale of assessments to finance the United Nations' budget in the General Assembly's fifth committee (2000–2001);
- focus on the relevance of the Economic and Social Council, deriving from the author's stewardship as its President in 2003;
- consider the internal politics involved in vying for elected posts in inter-governmental bodies, by focusing on the campaign to be elected to the Security Council between Guatemala and Venezuela in 2006;
- reflect on the peculiarities of decision-making in the Security Council.

Providing an insider's view on the UN and exploring a different facet of multilateral diplomacy at the UN this book will be of great use and interest to scholars of international relations and the diplomatic community.

Gert Rosenthal is a Guatemalan economist. He has alternated his career between public service in Guatemala and international organizations. He was Secretary-General of the National Planning Secretariat before joining the UN Economic Commission for Latin America and the Caribbean, where he served as Executive Secretary. After retiring from the UN secretariat he served as Permanent Representative of Guatemala to the UN, then as Foreign Minister, followed by a second tour to the UN to lead the Guatemalan delegation to the Security Council. He was the Chair of the Advisory Group of Experts for the 2015 review of the UN's peacebuilding architecture.

Global Institutions

Edited by Thomas G. Weiss
The CUNY Graduate Center, New York, USA
and Rorden Wilkinson
University of Sussex, Brighton, UK

About the series

The "Global Institutions Series" provides cutting-edge books about many aspects of what we know as "global governance." It emerges from our shared frustrations with the state of available knowledge—electronic and print-wise, for research and teaching—in the area. The series is designed as a resource for those interested in exploring issues of international organization and global governance. And since the first volumes appeared in 2005, we have taken significant strides toward filling conceptual gaps.

The series consists of three related "streams" distinguished by their blue, red, and green covers. The blue volumes, comprising the majority of the books in the series, provide user-friendly and short (usually no more than 50,000 words) but authoritative guides to major global and regional organizations, as well as key issues in the global governance of security, the environment, human rights, poverty, and humanitarian action among others. The books with red covers are designed to present original research and serve as extended and more specialized treatments of issues pertinent for advancing understanding about global governance. And the volumes with green covers—the most recent departure in the series—are comprehensive and accessible accounts of the major theoretical approaches to global governance and international organization.

The books in each of the streams are written by experts in the field, ranging from the most senior and respected authors to first-rate scholars at the beginning of their careers. In combination, the three components of the series—blue, red, and green—serve as key resources for faculty, students, and practitioners alike. The works in the blue and green streams have value as core and complementary readings in courses on, among other things, international organization, global governance, international law, international relations, and international political economy; the red volumes allow further reflection and investigation in these and related areas.

The books in the series also provide a segue to the foundation volume that offers the most comprehensive textbook treatment available dealing with all the major issues, approaches, institutions, and actors in contemporary global governance—our edited work *International Organization and Global Governance* (2014)—a volume to which many of the authors in the series have contributed essays.

Understanding global governance—past, present, and future—is far from a finished journey. The books in this series nonetheless represent significant steps toward a better way of conceiving contemporary problems and issues as well as, hopefully, doing something to improve world order. We value the feedback from our readers and their role in helping shape the on-going development of the series.

A complete list of titles can be viewed online here: https://www.routledge.com/Global-Institutions/book-series/GI.

The most recent titles in the series are:

International Institutions of the Middle East (2017)
by James Worrall

The Politics of Expertise in International Organizations (2017)
edited by Annabelle Littoz-Monnet

Obstacles of Peacebuilding (2017)
by Graciana del Castillo

UN Peacekeeping Doctrine in a New Era (2017)
edited by Cedric de Coning, Chiyuki Aoi, and John Karlsrud

Global Environmental Institutions (2nd edition, 2017)
by Elizabeth R. DeSombre

Global Governance and Transnationalizing Capitalist Hegemony (2017)
by Ian Taylor

Human Rights and Humanitarian Intervention (2016)
edited by Elizabeth M. Bruch

Inside the United Nations
Multilateral Diplomacy Up Close

Gert Rosenthal

Routledge
Taylor & Francis Group

LONDON AND NEW YORK

First published 2017 by Routledge

2 Park Square, Milton Park, Abingdon, Oxfordshire OX14 4RN
52 Vanderbilt Avenue, New York, NY 10017

Routledge is an imprint of the Taylor & Francis Group, an informa business

First issued in paperback 2018

British Library Cataloguing in Publication Data
A catalogue record for this book is available from the British Library

Library of Congress Cataloging in Publication Data
A catalog record for this book has been requested

ISBN: 978-1-138-23668-4 (hbk)
ISBN: 978-0-367-18888-7 (pbk)

Typeset in Times New Roman
by Taylor & Francis Books

Printed in the United Kingdom
by Henry Ling Limited

Contents

Table

Preface

I have spent almost 12 years representing Guatemala at the United Nations Headquarters in New York, in two separate tours of duty, 1999–2004 and 2008–2014. I came to the job without being a professional diplomat, having dedicated my entire career to development economics, both at home and in international organizations. When I was invited in 1999 to take on this new responsibility, I gathered that it was on the basis of my previous experience as Executive Secretary of the United Nations' Economic Commission for Latin America and the Caribbean (ECLAC) during the preceding ten years. Presumably, the offer was made under the assumption that I must have learned something about multilateral diplomacy along the way.

Truth be told, I was very reluctant to accept the invitation, having absorbed a bit of the bureaucratic arrogance that is displayed by many Latin American technocrats in the economic policy establishment: we tend to take a rather dim view of the foreign policy professionals and their craft. Happily, it was my wife, Margit, who convinced me to give it a try: she had followed me to Guatemala, Mexico and Chile during 38 years, so now we were faced with the opportunity of spending an interlude in her country of citizenship for the first time in our married life. It turned out to be a good call. Outside of the delights of living in New York, I found the work to be fascinating and rewarding. More importantly, it gave me the opportunity to better understand the intergovernmental process of decision making which shapes what the United Nations, in all its complexity, actually does to make it function.

With time, my disdain for diplomats turned to admiration, especially for a relatively small cadre of very talented individuals with whom I had the privilege of working as colleagues. In addition, my background in economic policy and management turned out to be a major asset for a diplomat; in fact, a double asset. First, the fact that I had worked for many years in senior posts within the secretariat gave me insights to its inner workings and bureaucratic culture that greatly facilitated my work at the intergovernmental level, given my close contacts with previous colleagues (including Kofi Annan, by then Secretary-General). After all, the way the intergovernmental organs and the secretariat interact is an essential component of multilateral diplomacy. Second, as one of the very few permanent representatives with an economic background, I was immediately mobilized to take on leadership roles within the intergovernmental structures in addressing development issues. This allowed the mission of Guatemala to assume an outsized role in the organization's development activities, and, at a more personal level, permitted me privileged positions which kept me fully active, gave me access to a wealth of information, exposed me to diverse and detailed experiences, and gave me the satisfaction of achieving what I believed to be tangible results.

Several colleagues and friends have suggested that I reflect about my varied exposures to the United Nations, both from within the secretariat and from the intergovernmental vantage points. However, I have resisted the idea of writing "my *memoires*" for several reasons. The first is that, with few and restricted exceptions, I never kept detailed records or diaries of my activities for posterity's sake, since I did not consider myself important enough to warrant such conceit. Although I tended to keep most documents and some correspondence that I found relevant at the time, when the clutter at home or in my office became unmanageable I went through fits of discarding everything in sight, which I now regret. A second reason is that I harbor serious doubts that anyone outside of my immediate circle of friends and family, and perhaps a small group of "UN watchers," mostly among delegates and in academia, would have much interest in what I have to say about my passage through the United Nations.

On the other hand, I did have to ask myself if my cumulative learning experience of so many years had left any "lessons learned" worthy of being shared with others. In this respect, it gradually dawned on me that there was at least one area of the United Nations that is insufficiently studied and even less understood. That is the inner dynamics of the intergovernmental machinery, its engagement with the secretariat, and how multilateral diplomacy actually functions in such a complex and multifaceted organization. My varied activities during the 12-year period had offered me advantageous observatories in all three of the main intergovernmental organs of the United Nations where policy decisions are crafted and adopted: the General Assembly, the Economic and Social Council, and the Security Council. Each of these organs has different responsibilities and distinct modalities of decision-making, and I had an insider's role as a direct participant of the dynamics at play.

Those dynamics are intricate, and do not respond to easy categorization. They involve many factors, some totally random, such as the personalities involved in any particular negotiation. But the general notion that member states, collectively, are the decision-makers, while the secretariat carries out their instructions and is accountable to them, is simply too abstract. Many consultations and negotiations are going on simultaneously, between individual member states, between those member states with the secretariat, and with outside stakeholders, such as NGOs, civil society, academics, parliamentarians, and the business sector. So, the reason I wrote this book was to capitalize on six specific experiences—or "case studies"—in which I played a protagonist role, with the idea of shedding some light on the permanent and diverse levels of engagement that make up the practice of multilateral diplomacy at the United Nations. In this, there seems to be a useful story to be told, while relatively little appears to be written on the matter, except for the occasional personal *memoirs* that touch on it, mostly in an anecdotal manner. The caveat is that the six cases explored cover unique events and during a limited time span, more akin to snapshots in contrast to a continuous film.

The narratives are meant to illustrate some of the parameters at play in the dynamics of consensus-building—virtually a synonym for decision-making—at the United Nations. They are by no means meant to offer a "blue book" on how to engage in multilateral diplomacy. Even less are the narratives conceived as a memoir, although they necessarily reflect a personal perspective and a distillation of the author's own "take-aways" of having spent a prolonged period dedicated to multilateral diplomacy. At any rate, this is not meant to be a monograph about the author, but rather a monograph about the United Nations and its inner-workings.

Antigua, Guatemala, August 2016

Abbreviations

ACT	Accountability Coherence and Transparency Group
ALBA	Spanish acronym for Bolivarian Alliance for the Peoples of Our America
AU	African Union
CARICOM	Caribbean Community
CELAC	Spanish acronym for Community of Latin American and Caribbean States
DESA	Department of Economic and Social Affairs
DFS	Department of Field Support
DPA	Department of Political Affairs
DPKO	Department of Peacekeeping Operations
DPR	Deputy Permanent Representative
DSG	Deputy Secretary-General
E10	Elected members of the Security Council
ECLAC	Economic Commission for Latin America and the Caribbean
ECOSOC	Economic and Social Council
ECOWAS	Economic Community of West African States
EU	European Union
FFD	Financing for Development
FOSS	Forum of small states
G4	Group of four countries, Brazil, Germany, India and Japan, advocating for expansion of the number of permanent members of the Security Council
G77	Group of Seventy Seven (now 131 developing countries) and China
GNP	Gross National Product
GRULAC	Group of Latin American and Caribbean States
HIPC	Heavily Indebted Poor Countries
IFIS	International Financial Institutions

ICGLR	International Conference on the Great Lakes Region
ICTR	International Criminal Tribunal for Rwanda
ICTY	International Criminal Tribunal for the former Yugoslavia
IGAD	Intergovernmental Authority on Development
IGN	Intergovernmental Negotiation process
JCC	Joint Coordinating Committee (between G77 and NAM)
LDC	Least Developed Country
NAM	Non-Aligned Movement
MDGs	Millennium Development Goals
OCHA	Office for Coordination of Humanitarian Affairs
ODA	Official Development Assistance
op	Operative paragraph
OHCHR	Office of the High Commissioner of Human Rights
OHCR	Office of the High Commissioner of Refugees
P5	Permanent members of the Security Council
PGA	President of the General Assembly
PSC	Peace and Security Council of the African Union
PR	Permanent Representative to the United Nations
Río Group	A regional grouping of eight Latin American countries (Argentina, Brazil, Colombia, Panamá, Perú, México, Uruguay and Venezuela), precursor of CELAC
SPM	Special Political Missions
SRSG	Special Representative of the Secretary-General
SWAPO	South West Africa People's Organization
UFC	United for Consensus (Group opposing expansion of Security Council in both categories)
UK	United Kingdom
UN	United Nations
UNCTAD	United Nations Conference on Trade and Development
UNDP	United Nations Development Programme
UNICEF	United Nations Children's Fund
UNOWA	United Nations Office for West Africa
UNTAG	United Nations Transition Assistance Group (in Namibia)
US	United States
WEOG	The Western European and Others Group

Introduction

- **The general context**
- **The organization of the United Nations' work**
- **An overview of the monograph**

The United Nations suggests different images to diverse observers. Its paradigms are expressed, among other aspects, in the work of UNICEF with children, the singular role of peacekeepers and the more general role of maintaining international peace, the growing presence of humanitarian assistance in man-made or natural disasters, advocacy for gender equality, the defense and promotion of human rights, the provision of services in various areas (such as health, education, agriculture, and technology); the publication of indicators, statistics, and analysis on a great variety of topics; support for development activities, even at the grass-roots level; norm-setting, from law of the sea to climate change, and many other subjects.

The concrete results of these diverse manifestations have certainly been mixed, and can be criticized for numerous shortcomings. But in general there appears to be recognition among member states and the broader constituency of the United Nations—"the people"—that the Organization has, on balance, been a positive presence ever since its creation, while the blue and white emblem of the United Nations still tends to command respect in most places of the world. Perhaps equally or more important, the noble ideal behind the United Nations, as expressed in the prologue of its Charter, is a highly compelling one, as relevant today as it was in 1945.

But there is another paradigm of the United Nations, symbolized by what goes on at its gleaming (and recently renovated) headquarters in New York (and, to a lesser extent, in Geneva and Vienna) where member states, the secretariat, and non-member stakeholders engage in an intricate minuet to give the organization a sense of direction as well as concrete "marching orders" in its diverse endeavors. This engagement has various expressions. Sometimes it has intrinsic value, as a wide variety of topics are debated—talking is always preferable to the outbreak of violence—and as the debate impacts on the tone, content, and shaping of the international agenda. But on other occasions the product of the debate leads to concrete actions, as the collective decisions of member states are codified in mandates contained in resolutions. Indeed, as "insiders" know full well, but the public at large often does not, the United Nations is the sum of all the parties concerned; namely, the member states and the secretariat; the latter embodied by the Secretary-General. The dynamics of this complex engagement—between member states and among member states and the secretariat—are the essence of multilateral diplomacy at the United Nations.[1]

The general context

This monograph offers some examples of how the aforementioned amalgam is fashioned, so a very short review of context is in order. The above-mentioned minuet is shaped by the Charter—the world body's constitution, as it were—which loosely defines the functions and powers of the principal intergovernmental organs and of the secretariat, complemented by detailed rules of procedures and gradually evolving norms and practices which define its working methods.[2] Over the lifetime of the organization, at least five distinct features have made those working methods ever more complex and time-consuming.

Expanding membership

The first reflects the fact that the membership evolved from the 51 original signatories to 193 at the time of writing, making consensus-building, at least in the General Assembly, increasingly cumbersome. Many delegations have tried to mitigate this trend by dealing with contentious issues in designated working groups of limited size, much as occurs with committees in legislative bodies. However, national legislatures are made up of a restricted number of political parties, which are represented in all committees. In contrast, at the United Nations sovereign states are often reluctant to delegate in others the responsibility of decision-making, even in its initial stages. Therefore the practice of designating smaller groupings, tasked to seek approximations to consensus before bringing the topic to the full membership, is resisted by many delegations. The latter argue that all matters should be worked out, discussed, and negotiated in plenary sessions, sacrificing agility for the sake of transparency and a sense of ownership on the part of all concerned.

Expansion of the international agenda

The second feature is that the agenda of the three principal inter-governmental organs, and especially the General Assembly, has grown exponentially over time. New topics deemed important are juxtaposed over preexisting topics, where there is frequently a constituency—sometimes large, often minuscule—that insists on maintaining a parti-cular topic open for consideration, even when its relevance has long been superseded. This has led to a proliferation of resolutions, where virtually the same text on any particular matter is approved year after year (or sometimes biennially), with minor modifications, making "previously agreed language" something only short of sacrosanct, and introducing an excessive element of ritual into the negotiation process.

Tensions between continuity and change

The third feature is derived from the fact that the United Nations recently celebrated its 70th anniversary, and, exaggerating somewhat just to make the point, a gradual process of sclerosis has set in, both at the level of the secretariat and at the intergovernmental level. Old practices tend to solidify, and the resistance to change is often fueled by different constituencies and interest groups that are permanently defending their institutional or even personal agenda and turf.

On the other hand, it is equally true that the United Nations has been constantly evolving over time, as is made clear in various chapters of this monograph. However, few people will dispute that it is difficult to achieve meaningful change in the decision-making process. When the manner of conducting business does evolve or adapt to changing circumstances, it tends to happen by incremental stages, rather than as a result of bold holistic transformations. At any rate, there is a clear and permanent tension between inertia shaping events in contrast to events overcoming inertia and forcing change. Stated differently, there is a permanent tension between continuity and change.

An inherent quality of multilateral diplomacy

In addition to the changes over time that have made consensus-building more difficult, there is an inherent attribute of multilateral diplomacy that should be stressed: to achieve consensus, or at least leaving all parties reasonably satisfied with any given decision, they all have to show some capacity to compromise. This reality tends to move decisions in the direction of the minimum common denominator between maximalist and minimalist solutions. That is why many observers find typical United Nations resolutions (notably at the level of the General Assembly) as too heavy in florid phrases and too light in substance as far as tangible actions are concerned, as well as more concerned with aspirations than actual results. And, of course, if instructions or policy guidance coming from the top are muddled and unclear in key areas such as priority-setting, defining "who does what" within the United Nations System, and setting standards and guidelines of accountability, the above mentioned attributes tends to be reflected at the level of the secretariat.

The expanding membership's distinct "pecking order"

One of the undeniable strengths of the United Nations is its universal nature; i.e. virtually all the countries on the planet are members. The Charter is based on the principle of sovereign equality of all its member states. But in the real world there are numerous metrics that establish a sort of "pecking order" among those members, including their population, their geographic extension, their wealth, their economic, financial, cultural, or military prowess, and many other factors which influence the degree of leverage they can exert on the outcome of multilateral decisions. The implicit "pecking order" is another permanent feature of multilateral diplomacy, as some delegations wrestle with real or perceived handicaps in bringing their positions to bear in multi-country negotiations. Since the author comes from a relatively small country,[3] this topic comes up repeatedly in the different chapters of this monograph, and especially in the one pertaining to the Security Council, where the implicit "pecking order" is explicitly institutionalized between permanent and elected members.

The organization of the United Nations' work

Another permanent feature of consensus building at the intergovernmental level, and especially at the General Assembly, is related to the way the work is organized and structured. As is well known, while the General Assembly conducts some of its work in its plenary sessions, most of it is undertaken first in one of its six main committees, organized around specialized areas (disarmament; economic and financial; social, humanitarian and cultural; special political and decolonization;

administrative and budgetary; and legal). In contrast to committees in national legislative bodies, all of these main committees have universal membership, and all elevate their decisions and recommendations to the plenary for approval. While they are designed to accelerate the work of the General Assembly, they also introduce additional layers of negotiation and especially new actors to the process. The specialists that cover any particular committee naturally represent their delegation's position, but they also tend to develop a peculiar affinity with their peers, which can translate into nuanced differences with their original instructions which sometimes have to be sorted out subsequently at the level of their respective mission. This is particularly true of the fifth committee, which deals with highly specialized topics which permanent representatives tend to delegate in their experts, who in turn tend to create an aura of mystery around their work which intimidates non-experts from intervening.

The organization of the intergovernmental organs' work is also influenced by some time-bound customs. While the President of the General Assembly (PGA) is elected on a yearly basis and is joined by 21 vice-presidents, the subsidiary bodies of both the General Assembly and of the Economic and Social Council (ECOSOC) have bureaus made up by a president, three vice-presidents, and a *rapporteur*, each representing one of the five regional groupings of member states on a rotating basis. The culmination of most decisions is codified in a formal outcome document, usually a resolution or a decision. To assist in the elaboration of a text, the bureau normally designates one or two facilitators whose role is not only to moderate the discussions, but to take an active role in seeking common ground between the different delegations. For its part, the Security Council has a rotating presidency (by alphabetical order in the English alphabet), whereby each member, permanent or elected, occupies the chair for one month.

Another characteristic of the dynamics of decision-making and implementation at Headquarters is a somewhat geocentric mindset, in that many of the actors think of the United Nations in terms of what is going on in New York and Geneva in terms of policy guidance, when most of the tangible results of their endeavors can only be tested by their impact "in the field." The somewhat negative stereotype of puffed-up ambassadors and their staffs in endless debates in the plush halls of New York stands in marked contrast to the more positive stereotype of peacekeepers, humanitarian aid workers, development advocates, or even national policy-makers working on the ground, where the action is. Of course, in the real world, neither stereotype reflects reality, but these images shape the way the world often perceives the United Nations, for better or for worse, and those perceptions then retro-feed into the dynamics of decision-making at the Organization.

Some of the general circumstances outlined above offer the parameters of what makes multilateral diplomacy at the United Nations so varied and complex. There are simply too many variables at play. An additional factor to take into account is that, over time, new stakeholders have emerged. Some of these are advocates for diverse and mostly worthy causes, and tend to behave much as lobbyists would act towards a legislative body: by pressing their agendas. The number of formally recognized NGOs has grown exponentially over the years, and the business sector has taken on a more pro-active role, especially with the creation of the Global Compact.[4] The presence of non-state stakeholders has in itself become an issue, with most member states welcoming this development, but many, representing less open regimes, resisting the trend, arguing that the United Nations is an organization made up exclusively of member states.

It should not come as a surprise, then, that the content, scope, and tone of consensus building varies considerably, depending on the subject matter, the different interests at play, and even the personalities that participate in any particular negotiation. The dynamics can also change over time, as a function of shifting circumstances and context. Further, the way decisions are shaped and taken to fruition is quite different in the Security Council, with its limited membership and peculiar system of governance, than it is in the General Assembly or in ECOSOC, as will be illustrated in subsequent chapters.

An overview of the monograph

The author has selected six specific case studies to illustrate some of the main elements of these dynamics. This is because specific cases clarify two important aspects of multilateral diplomacy in a more compelling manner than general characterizations. First, they offer concrete examples of the numerous ingredients that ultimately shape decision-making in a multilateral setting. Second, they confirm the oft-repeated phrase that excludes "one size fits all" formulas for consensus-building. Each case presented has unique characteristics.

There is no particular reason for having selected those specific cases instead of others that could have been equally revealing, except for the fact that the author had a front-row seat to witness the dynamics at play. Those cases are presented in more-or-less chronological order (the exception is Chapter 2, which occupies its place due to its subject matter being closely linked to that of Chapter 1). It should be recalled that the "insider's view"—"up close" mentioned in the title—is an important element of this monograph.

It should also be noted that the distinct features mentioned in the preceding pages appear as cross-cutting issues in each and every case study. Of these, four refer to explicit consensus-building exercises attached to singular issues addressed by the General Assembly. They offer the breadth and scope of what the United Nations does. Chapters 1 and 2 cover the origin and preparation of two exceptionally successful international conferences; the latter are among the many tools in the arsenal of multilateral diplomacy. Emphasis is placed on the interaction between the intergovernmental organ and the secretariat in achieving a meaningful outcome of the conferences. More specifically: the first case deals with the preparatory process and outcome of the 2000 Millennium Summit, which led to the subsequent adoption of the Millennium Development Goals (MDGs). The second refers to the preparatory process and the outcome of the 2002 International Conference on Financing for Development held in Monterrey, Mexico.

Chapter 3 changes course, and takes a look at a particularly contentious negotiation on the scale of assessments to finance the United Nations' budget in the General Assembly's fifth committee during its 55th session (2000–2001). It provides an inside look at the work of one of the General Assembly's main committees, and, more broadly, explores how member states finance the budget of the United Nations, as well as the dynamics behind agreeing on the allocations of expenditures.

Chapter 4 is derived from the author's stewardship of the Economic and Social Council as its president in 2003, and is focused on the relevance of this organ. It explores the linkages between the principal intergovernmental organs. An important paradox that is raised is that ECOSOC, which is assigned specific functions in the Charter to coordinate UN efforts in the development field, is itself a victim of the fragmentation that characterizes the United Nations, since the functions of the Council and the General Assembly strongly overlap.

Chapter 5 takes a close look at another aspect of multilateral diplomacy at the United Nations: the internal politics involved in vying for elected posts in the various intergovernmental bodies. It narrates the tumultuous outcome of a campaign to be elected to the Security Council in 2006 between Guatemala and Venezuela, which went through 47 rounds of balloting before a final outcome played out.

Chapter 6 contains some reflections on the peculiarities of decision-making in the Security Council, especially as perceived from the perspective of a smaller member state, and offers some insights to the internal workings of what is surely the world's most important multilateral organ.

Each of the chapters dedicated to these topics explores a different facet of multilateral diplomacy at the United Nations, and some common threads are pulled together in the final chapter, under the heading of "lessons learned."

Notes

1 The author did not think it necessary to go into the definitions of "multi-lateralism," "diplomacy," or "multilateral diplomacy," although there are nuanced differences in how diverse analysts understand these terms. Its conventional meaning is the practice of involving more than two nations or parties in achieving diplomatic solutions to common supranational problems.

2 When alluding to the principal intergovernmental organs, these consist today of the General Assembly, the Economic and Social Council, and the Security Council, since the Trusteeship Council's initial successes eventually led to its virtual abolishment by 1994.

3 No effort is made to define the scope of a "small country," although some years ago Singapore established an informal grouping named the Forum of Small States (FOSS), which includes all countries whose population is below 10 million. At the United Nations, "smallness" is a relative concept ("small" in relation to other countries) and is a result of a combination of several factors, including not only size and wealth, but also the quality of the for-eign policy establishment and how proactive any given country becomes. A current example of the latter is that Ambassador Peter Thomson of Fiji (population: 900,000) is the President of the 71st session of the General Assembly.

4 See: www.unglobalcompact.org.

1 The 2000 Millennium Declaration
A General Assembly Summit with far-reaching consequences

- The genesis
- The next stage
- The preparatory process
- The final phase
- The Millennium Summit
- The Coda
- Conclusion

The decision to hold some type of commemoration in the year 2000, announcing not only a new century but a new millennium, was taken on 17 December 1998, when the General Assembly adopted resolution 53/202, whereby member states decided to designate the 55th session of the General Assembly "The Millennium Assembly of the United Nations." At that time, they decided to convene, as an integral part of the Millennium Assembly of the United Nations, a Millennium Summit on dates to be decided by the General Assembly at its resumed fifty-third session, under the presidency of Didier Opertti, the foreign minister of Uruguay. The only guideline offered by resolution 53/202 was that the event should be held during "a limited number of days." All other aspects, such as dates, level of representation, format, thematic content, and potential outcome, had to be worked out by member states, presumably by consensus. Hence, the need for facilitators: the traditional way of getting the broad membership to agree on difficult issues. PGA Opertti asked the author and Michael Powles, the Permanent Representative of New Zealand, to take on that responsibility. This turned out to be a standard beginning for anything but a standard outcome of a gathering that was to have far-reaching consequences.

The genesis

As a first step, the co-facilitators invited a limited number of key dele-gates to informal consultations in the format of what was called a "coordination committee." These consultations were held between 13 and 16 April 1999, and included the permanent representatives of Germany (representing the European Union (EU) at the time), Guyana (representing the Group of 77 and China (G77)), South Africa (representing the Non-aligned Movement (NAM)), Uganda (chairman of the African Group), Algeria, Australia, Brazil, Canada, China, Cuba, Egypt, France, India, Japan, Mexico, Pakistan, Romania, the Russian Federation, the United States, and Sweden. This informal committee was a way of overcoming the resistance on the part of many member states to discuss important matters outside of the plenary or committees made up of universal membership. President Opertti was eager to nail down a date for the event, as well as its duration. Based on the consultations, the co-facilitators could report back to him on 21 April that most of the delegations participating in the coordination committee were close to agreement on the meaning of "a limited number of days" as a minimum of two and a maximum of four. On the timing, the majority preferred holding the event immediately before or during the general debate, although Germany (representing the EU), Japan, and China indicated a preference for the first week of December 1999, during the 54th session.

There had also been a rather loose discussion of other elements, such as thematic content, format, and outcome, but here there was a wider disparity of positions, with some delegates expressing doubts as to whether an outcome document should even be pursued. This seemed strange to the author, given the symbolic significance of the event, but there was always some resistance on the part of a limited number of delegations to preparing lengthy political declarations, given the time and effort that their preparation entailed.

In May 1999 the Secretary-General himself weighed in on some of these matters in a report which contains specific recommendations on the over-arching theme and sub-topics which he believed could facil-itate the debate of the General Assembly.[1] This report followed the usual pattern of the secretariat exercising its responsibility of for-mulating proposals, which, in its judgment, were appropriate for the circumstances at hand, but which offered the member states some leeway in putting together a collective decision, usually based on con-sensus, but sometimes adopted through the alternative of putting the text to a vote.

The next stage

By the end of May 1999, PGA Opertti managed to convene two informal consultations of the plenary, and he at least got a decision on dates, reflected in resolution 53/239 adopted on 8 June 1999. This resolution indicated that the Summit would begin on Wednesday 6 September 2000. Two other decisions were taken. First, an initial approximation on format was agreed to, in that the Summit would be composed of plenary meetings and of four interactive round-table sessions. Second, the Summit would be co-chaired by the incoming PGA of the 55th session as well as the outgoing PGA of the 54th session, under whose watch most of the preparatory phase would take place. However, President Opertti was unable to get a consensus on the duration of the Summit, although the overwhelming majority of delegations accepted the proposition of a three-day event. The inability to reach a consensual decision is what led to a typical tactic of multilateral diplomacy: to postpone the decision while further consultations take place.

The discussion of other matters, such as a more detailed development of the format, the thematic content, the participation of non-state actors, and the nature and content of the outcome was left for the preparatory process to be launched during the 54th session of the General Assembly, under the Presidency of Theo-Ben Gurirab, the foreign minister of Namibia, who took over his duties on 14 September 1999.

The preparatory process

Theo-Ben Gurirab was an imposing figure.[2] In his past, he was an activist in the South West Africa People's Organization (SWAPO). Part of his political activities took him into a protracted exile (mostly in the United States). During that period he rose in the liberation movement's ranks, and he eventually became the head of the SWAPO mission based in New York, mostly to engage with the United Nations. In the final stages of SWAPO's initiatives, and back in his home country, he became one of the main drafters of Namibia's Constitution as a member of the Constituent Assembly prior to independence. He became the first Minister of Foreign Affairs of the newly independent country in 1990.[3] His personal attributes added to the luster of Namibia, which, it will be recalled, acquired its independence from South Africa while the latter still was ruled by apartheid. The United Nations played an important role in Namibia's independence process,[4] including the establishment of the United Nations Transition Assistance Group (UNTAG) under Marti Ahtisaari. In short, when Mr. Gurirab assumed the presidency, he already found a deep well of sympathy, for himself and for his country.

The two co-facilitators were summoned to Mr. Gurirab's office shortly after his taking over the presidency of the 54th Session. They were asked to continue co-facilitating the preparatory process for the Millennium Summit, and invited to participate in a substantive meeting with his senior staff to discuss a preliminary work program. It was understood that the preparatory process would only get into high-gear after the regular business of the session was concluded, presumably by mid-December. Further, the Secretary-General had promised to have his own report with proposals for a Summit outcome by early March 2000, roughly six months before the holding of the event. This report was to be an essential input for the preparatory process, and therefore became an important marker in the work program's calendar. In the meantime, some activities were carried out during the last quarter of 1999 under the new presidency, especially since member states seemed to be devoting as much if not more attention to the organizational aspects of the Summit than to its substantial outcome.

Among the issues being debated was the format, or how to organize the debate. Was this to be a celebratory event which would put the accent on what the United Nations had done in the past, or a practical event, which could offer a vision of the role of the United Nations for the future? There were different views on the matter. As to format, the extreme positions were, on the one hand, that plenary sessions were a waste of time, dedicated to ritualistic speeches, and that the UN should for once organize a real inter-active discussion on pressing issues that could shape the unrealized potential of the organization. On the other hand, arguments were put forth that heads of state could not be expected to make the long journey to New York if they weren't offered a stage to speak, mostly for the sake of their domestic constituencies, and that purported inter-active discussions would anyway end up as a series of formal prepared statements.

As often happens during the consensus-building process, an intermediate solution was reached on this matter through a combination of plenary meetings and round tables; the only difficulty in finding common ground between opposing views was in the division of time between the two types of gathering.[5] In addition, there was also the issue of themes for the inter-active round tables: should they all discuss the same topic, or should they be organized around different subjects? And what procedures would be implemented to distribute different countries to one of the four round tables? A further particularly contentious issue was how the Chairs of these round tables would be selected.

Much of the time of the co-facilitators, and even of President Gurirab, was dedicated to listening to different positions and trying to find enough common ground so as to come out with a consensus. It was the PGA's intention to reach such a consensus by February 2000; in fact, the agreement was only reached on 11 August, when the General Assembly adopted resolution 54/281, called "Organization of the Millennium Summit of the United Nations." The gap in the two dates only illustrated that even in procedural matters it is difficult to garner consensus, and more often than not the "spoilers" or hold-outs elect the stratagem of going down to the wire rather than giving up on their favored positions.

During the first half of 2000, the organizational aspects were discussed simultaneously with the substantive matters, and each set of discussions impacted on the other. As already noted, when consultations were begun during the 53rd session, many delegations resisted the idea of a formal declaration coming out of the Summit, although the prevailing opinion was that such a solemn gathering would be meaningless without a tangible outcome document. But the content of such a document had to be accompanied by other decisions, such as whether it should take the form of a presidential summary, a resolution of the General Assembly, a political declaration of the heads of state, or a combination of these and other options.

The facilitators, for their part, had initiated at that time discreet consultations with the secretariat to sound out the Secretary-General's own aspirations for the event. Besides very occasional meetings with the Secretary-General himself, more frequent conversations were held with the Deputy Secretary-General, Louise Frechette, who had been designated to oversee the process on the secretariat's side.[6] And a superior working relationship was developed with John Ruggie, who, in his capacity as Assistant Secretary-General for Strategic Planning, and with the help of Andrew Mack, was heading the team drafting the Secretary-General's promised report, which was meant to guide the discussions on the outcome of the summit.

The long-awaited report was finally issued on 27 March 2000, under the title *"We the peoples: the role of the United Nations in the twenty-first century."*[7] It was a lucid, ambitious, visionary, and very well-drafted document, which bore the substantive stamp of John Ruggie and the formal editing skills of Edward Mortimer, the director of communications of the Secretary-General's executive office. It was, in fact, destined to become a landmark document of the secretariat, and it also became the basis of the very first draft declarations that the co-facilitators eventually produced.

The President of the General Assembly convened several informal consultations of the plenary, often with his personal participation, sometimes only with the presence of the two co-facilitators. General comments were received on the contents of the Secretary General's report, and then more specific comments on the recommendations contained therein. These consultations were held in April and May 2000. Although reactions to the report were, in general, quite positive regarding its conceptual framework, as well as its structure, contents, and proposals, it also became clear in the course of these meetings that numerous delegations had their own ideas and agendas for a declaration. Many comments referred to what were perceived as serious omissions. Thus, there was always the latent danger that the very brief declaration that both the secretariat and the PGA were looking for—President Gurirab spoke frequently of a "brisk" text—would gradually be expanded to accommodate the initiatives of different delegations. In order to avoid this risk, the president announced to the plenary that he would present an initial draft declaration—he called it a "non-paper"—built on the Secretary-General's Report and on the content of the numerous interventions of member states.

That "non-paper" was prepared during the first week of June, in two phases. During the first phase, a text was developed by the two co-facilitators, who then turned it over both to the PGA and the secretariat (in the person of John Ruggie). In the second phase, the comments, observations, and suggestions received from these two sources were brought into the text, which was then circulated among delegates in mid-June. With the benefit of hindsight, it is heartening to note that the final version of the Millennium Declaration is actually quite close to this initial "non-paper." However, during the brief ensuing period between the consideration of the first and last draft, the text went through some significant mutations, as the PGA and co-facilitators tried to address differing concerns of delegations. These efforts were having, in balance, a deleterious effect on the evolving draft, which began to expand in length and was losing the "crispness" sought by the PGA. Further, the inner coherence of the original non-paper was gradually being compromised, as suggested modifications from the different delegations were brought into succeeding versions. Still, up to the end of July, a line-by-line revision of the text had been averted, precisely to maintain the coherence of the Declaration.

The final phase

The President's next draft proposal (the natural extension of the previous "non-paper"), which presumably had addressed at least the general concerns raised during the consultations of previous weeks, was circulated on 10 August. It was the PGA's intention to invite comments to the text, again without going into a paragraph-by-paragraph revision, and offered to come back to the plenary with a revised version which, he hoped, would be acceptable to all delegations. The co-facilitators had already been alerted as to the most controversial paragraphs, so some preemptive actions were taken in the preparation of the text, addressing different concerns and proposals presented during the consultations. In a few instances, specific delegations were approached to consult the wording of paragraphs that they had expressed particular interest in.

When the next draft was put to the plenary, there still were observations and proposals surrounding some of the more contentious aspects, but the distance between different positions had definitely been narrowed. A revised text was offered which would address the new or reiterated concerns expressed, and it was circulated during the third week of August. President Gurirab went out on a limb, and put his personal stamp on the text, asking delegations to accept it as a consensus document. Not all delegations were willing to do so, but in the end the PGA prevailed, given the considerable prestige he had acquired during his tenure and the forceful manner in which he chaired the last plenary.

Thus, the text was approved by the informal consultations, and then adopted by the General Assembly, still as a draft, on 5 September as resolution 54/282, which decided "to refer the annexed draft United Nations Millennium Declaration to the Millennium Summit of the United Nations ... for its consideration." This is the same text that was finally adopted by the Summit on 8 September (resolution 55/2). It indeed turned out to be "short and crisp", reflecting in its 32 paragraphs a vision for the United Nation's role in the twenty-first century.

The Millennium Summit

The Millennium Summit evolved as expected. During the three days allotted to this event, and under the joint Presidency of Theo-Ben Gurirab and Harri Holkeri (President of the 55th session), all member states, which included 149 heads of state, had the opportunity to deliver 5-minute statements to the plenary and participate in one of four interactive round tables; the first time such an exercise had been held at UN summits or conferences.[8] Selected non-governmental organizations were also invited to participate in the debate. All four roundtables addressed the central theme of the challenges posed by globalization and how its potential adverse forces could be moderated. The first roundtable, held on the afternoon of 6 September, was chaired by Prime Minister Goh Chok Tong of Singapore. The second and third roundtables, held on 7 September (one in the morning, the other in the afternoon), were chaired by the Presidents of Poland and of Venezuela, Aleksander Kwasniewski and Hugo Chávez Frias, respectively. The last roundtable was held on the morning of 8 September and chaired by the President of Algeria, Abdelaziz Bouteflika. In the reports presented by the four Chairs during the final session of the plenary, all of them made a special point of the fact that they had found the debates extremely interesting and constructive.

The Coda

Consistent with the historical importance of the event, the Millennium Declaration had far-reaching consequences. Three months after the Summit took place, the General Assembly adopted resolution 55/162 dealing with the follow-up of the Declaration. Among other aspects, the Secretary-General was asked to prepare a report dealing with the fulfil-ment of the commitments contained in the Declaration. The requested report was issued on 6 September 2001 under the title "Road map towards the implementation of the United Nations Millennium Declaration" (A/56/326). This report sought to develop a comprehensive set of indi-cators reflected in the Millennium Declaration. Certain liberties were taken by the secretariat in drawing on commitments and targets adopted by member states in a series of global conferences held in the 1990s.[9] The secretariat then codified the Millennium Declaration into eight broad goals, which were spelled out in an annex to the report.[10]

These eight goals, supported by 18 quantified and time-bound tar-gets and 48 indicators, became known as the *Millennium Development Goals* (MDGs). They were meant to focus on measurable improve-ments not just for developing countries but for the countries that help fund development programs and for the multilateral institutions that help countries implement them. As is famously known, the goals were: eradicating extreme poverty and hunger; achieving universal primary education; promoting gender equality and empowering women; reducing child mortality; improving maternal health; combating HIV/AIDS, malaria and other diseases; ensuring environmental sustainability; and, to insure progress on all these fronts, building a global partnership for development.[11] In these high-priority areas, the MDGs mirrored the concerns of the secretariat's original proposal contained in *We the peoples: the role of the United Nations in the twenty-first century.*

By putting the first seven goals under a unified, holistic framework, and recognizing that their implementation was the primary responsi-bility of each country, but requiring international cooperation, the

Millennium Summit had an enormous impact on public awareness, and, more importantly, in the arenas of policy making and priority setting. There was a certain magic in repeating over and over again this focused and short list of major development goals, which began to inform the policies of both developing economies and the donor community, including the multilateral financial institutions, which adopted the MDG mantra as their own.

The General Assembly, for its part, assimilated the MDGs as part of the UN's lexicon. The concept was not endorsed outright for many years, due to concerns mainly of one delegation—the United States—that the commitments could be construed by some as binding obligations. That is why initially the Secretary-General's Report of 2001 was only received by "taking note with appreciation ..."[12] But with time even the United States started using the terminology of the MDGs, which became part of the legacy of the United Nations for the period, and an important framework for the work of the organization in the development field. Most developing countries assimilated the MDGs in their own development strategies, and regularly prepared reports on the progress achieved and the obstacles encountered in fulfilling their commitments.

As Kofi Annan rightly reflects in his own memoirs, "the MDGs soon became the overarching framework for the entire international development agenda ..."

> To anyone who reflects back on the agreement, there is no denying its significance. With all the partners that had morally and formally bought into the project alongside the member states, with the common interest of so many otherwise diverse communities around the world, this was more than just a breakthrough UN declaration: it bore the hallmarks of a global social movement.[13]

Conclusion

From the author's personal reflection, and with the benefit of hindsight, the preparatory process of the Millennium Summit was one of the more successful exercises of multilateral diplomacy undertaken at the United Nations in recent decades. For once, in 2000 all the stars appeared to be propitiously aligned. A symbolic occasion was offered for member states to reflect on what the United Nations had achieved since its founding, and to offer a vision for the work of the Organization on the dawn of a new millennium. The secretariat turned in a superior performance. In the first place, it produced an unusually compelling document to shape the discussions. Secondly, a superior working relationship was developed with the PGA and the co-facilitators in moving the process forward.[14] Member states also showed forbearance during the process, and especially in the final stages, in not insisting on their preferred national agendas. And clearly the whole process would not have come together so successfully had it not been for the exceptional leadership and drive shown by President Gurirab. Further, the Summit was the basis of the follow-up activities which spawned the MDGs, whose subsequent impact on development policies is broadly considered one of the United Nations' major achievements in recent decades.

A final reflection: at the time of writing this chapter, at the end of 2015, the target date for the MDGs, the United Nations adopted a more ambitious, more universal successor arrangement to the MDGs, under the banner of the Sustainable Development Goals, negotiated during 2014 and the first half of 2015, and reflected in a new United Nations summit for the adoption of the post-2015 development agenda, with the title *"Transforming our world: the 2030 Agenda for Sustainable Development."*[15] This new agenda, which contains 17 sustainable development goals and 169 associated targets, represent a normative shift towards a more comprehensive agenda that integrates the social, economic, and environmental dimensions of development, and includes a goal to "promote peaceful and inclusive societies for sustainable development, provide access to justice for all and build effective, accountable and inclusive institutions at all levels living in peace." It is also conceived as a universal agenda, as well as people-centered. It proposes—much as the *Popol Vuh*, the classic mythology of Western Guatemala's Mayan people—that "no one should be left behind."[16] This new Agenda could not have been developed and adopted without its predecessor discussed in this chapter.

Notes

1   A/53/948 of 10 May 1999, "The Millennium Assembly of the United Nations: Thematic Framework for the Millennium Summit."
2   See: www.un.org/General Assembly/54/session/bio.htm.
3   In 2002 Mr. Gurirab became prime minister of Namibia, a post he held until 2004.
4   See: Security Council resolution 435 (1978).
5   The issue was resolved in adopting resolution 53/239, 8 June 1999.
6   Kofi Annan, *Interventions: A Life in War and Peace* (New York: The Penguin Press, 2012), 226.
7   A/54/2000, 27 March 2000.

8 See: www.un.org/General Assembly/55/pvlista55.htm, verbatim records of 3rd to 8th plenary meetings, 6–8 September 2000.
9 These include: The World Summit for Children, New York, 1990; World Conference on Education for All, Jomtien, 1990; International Conference on Nutrition, Rome, 1992; United Nations Conference on Environment and Development, Rio de Janeiro, 1992; World Conference on Human Rights, Vienna, 1993; International Conference on Population and Development, Cairo, 1994; Global Conference on Small Island Developing States, Barbados, 1994; Fourth World Conference on Women, Beijing, China, 1995; World Summit on Social Development, Copemhagen, 1995; World Food Summit, Rome, 1996.
10 A/56/326, 56–58.
11 See: www.un.org/millenniumgoals.
12 Resolution 56/95, 14 December 2001, 1.
13 Annan, *Interventions: A Life in War and Peace*, 227.
14 It should be noted that Deputy Secretary-General Louise Frechette and ASG John Rugie played especially significant roles.
15 Resolution 70/1, 25 September 2015.
16 *Popol Vuh*, Part IV, Chapter 2, paragraph 10: "Arise, all of you, call everyone, let there be not one group, nor two groups, among us who remain behind the others."

2 The 2002 International Conference on Financing for Development

- **The first phase**
- **The second phase**
- **The third phase**
- **Conclusion**

The Millennium Declaration discussed in the previous chapter contains the following phrase issued by the heads of state: "We are concerned about the obstacles developing countries face in mobilizing the resources needed to finance their sustained development. We will therefore make every effort to ensure the success of the High-level International and Intergovernmental Event on Financing for Development, to be held in 2001."[1] Indeed, a discussion that had lasted almost a decade on the holding of such an event was nearing fruition. The long road towards what finally became the Monterrey conference, generally perceived to be one of the most successful events ever organized by the United Nations in the economic and social spheres, is a story worth recalling as another positive outcome of United Nations multilateral diplomacy. It would be tedious and unproductive to describe all the twists and turns encountered on the long road from its conception to its consummation. But a narrative that captures at least its general contours, its ups and downs, and the way the Consensus was gradually built, offers some important insights and lessons.

The road can be divided into three broad stages. The first, which roughly covers the period 1991 to 1998, falls in the category of the routine activities of the Economic and Social Council as well as the General Assembly to get a relatively simple idea off the ground, and give it some traction. The second, which covers the period 1998–1999, reveals a more focused effort to define the scope, content, agenda, and organization of "an event" on financing for development. This effort was led by an "Ad Hoc open-ended working group." The third phase, which covered the preparatory process and the actual holding of the event, covered the period 2000–2002, and was the one that had the most singular characteristics in terms of the dynamics of multilateral diplomacy at the United Nations. These three phases will be described and analyzed in more-or-less chronological order in the following pages.

The first phase

The first mention of a possible United Nations conference on development financing appeared in a statement delivered by Secretary-General Javier Pérez de Cuéllar at the opening of the second regular session of the Economic and Social Council of 1991. The idea was launched in the broader context of various member-driven initiatives especially dear to the developing countries, such as the "International Development Strategy for the Fourth United Nations Development Decade,"[2] and the "Declaration on International Economic Co-operation in particular the Revitalization of Economic Growth and Development of the Developing Countries," adopted during the 18th Special Session of the General Assembly.[3] The Economic and Social Council "took note" of the Secretary-General's proposal, and further decided that "consideration be given to the convening of an international conference on development financing and ... to refer the matter to the General Assembly at its forty-sixth session for further consideration."[4]

It appears that the Secretary-General's suggestion was not received with great enthusiasm by all members of ECOSOC, given the reluctance of the General Assembly to address the issue. Rather, the characteristic reaction of UN intergovernmental organs to highly controversial topics is to try and put off their consideration. In this particular case, the General Assembly decided to again postpone acting on the proposal until the 47th session.[5] Once more during the 47th session it could not bring itself to adopt a resolution, but rather decided to "continue exploring the issue in the 48th session."[6] As could have been predicted, during the 48th session it decided "to continue to explore the issue of the financing of development ..." and again deferred any decision until the 50th session.[7] When the 50th session rolled around, the decision taken was to consider the matter at the 52nd session.[8] Behind each of these decisions of postponement there were many hours of contentious discussion, mostly between developing countries of the "South" and developed countries of the "North." When those discussions led to a dead end, the only matter on which delegations could agree was to push the matter off for a new try in the future, basically to keep the initiative alive (albeit barely).

The overriding obstacle to moving ahead on the proposal was the stiff resistance in the early years on the part of some of the advanced economies to allow the United Nations to get involved in anything that smacked of finance: the treaty-mandated jurisdiction of the Bretton Woods Institutions. The G77, for its part, pushed back, invoking the Organization's central role in development, and arguing that it was impossible to debate development issues without bringing finance into the picture. This appeared to be a compelling argument, which gradually led to some common ground between developed and developing countries, based on putting development at the center of the discussion, but explored through the optic of financing.

So, in 1997, and after much procrastination, the General Assembly finally adopted a resolution entitled "Global partnership for development: high-level international intergovernmental consideration of financing for development", in which it took some concrete, although tentative steps by deciding to:

> convene a resumed session of the Second Committee of the fifty-second session for two days in order to solicit the views of Governments on the inputs required from a broad range of stakeholders, including actors both within and outside the United Nations system, as well as views on key elements that might be included in the consideration of the topic of financing for development, and to identify potential sources of such inputs.[9]

More importantly, the resolution mandated the creation of "an Ad Hoc open-ended working group to work during the fifty-third session of the General Assembly in order to undertake an in-depth examination of all the inputs requested, with a view to formulating a report containing recommendations on the form, scope, and agenda of the high-level international intergovernmental consideration of the topic of financing for development, which will be submitted to the General Assembly at its fifty-fourth session." It further decided "to consider at the fifty-fourth session of the General Assembly the convening, *inter alia*, of a summit, international conference, special session of the General Assembly or other appropriate high-level international intergovernmental forum on financing for development to further the global partnership for development, not later than the year 2001."[10] In short, the process was creeping forward, incrementally.

The second phase

Thus, a relatively clear two-year time-table was set up to move towards actually holding the long sought after conference. Persistence on the part of the G77 and forbearance on the part of the more developed countries had finally led to a minimum platform of agreements, and the foundations of a potential meeting had been laid. Those foundations were further developed during the 53rd session, when the General Assembly requested the president to serve as ex officio chairman of the ad hoc working group and invited him to designate two vice-chairs and to convene its organizational meeting in January 1999.[11]

The ad hoc open-ended working group of the General Assembly on financing for development held its organizational session on 17 December 1998, and approved a work program which contemplated three formal sessions for the first quarter of 1999, in addition to several informal sessions.[12] The first formal session was held from 9–11 February, followed by two informal meetings on 16–19 March and 5–8 April, respectively, to review each of the "major elements" or topics that had been proposed by the Secretary-General in his report A/53/470. The second formal session was held on 4 May to receive the reports of the prior informal meetings, which in turn were discussed in two additional informal meetings held on 12–14 May and 27 May. The third and final session was held on 28 May.[13] The bureau of the General Assembly's second committee, complying with the mandate contained in resolution 52/179, also held informal consultations with business leaders and non-governmental organizations. The dates of those gathering were 15 March and 1 April 1999, respectively.

Many substantive issues, as well as the general thrust of the scope, agenda, and format of a prospective conference were progressively being clarified by the evolving discussions held on this matter since the beginning of the decade in the Economic and Social Council and in the General Assembly, added to informal consultations with member states and other stakeholders, specific studies commissioned with academics and contributions from UN specialized agencies and especially the World Bank. Towards the end of the decade, a specialized web site was established to make this material easily available to delegates and other interested parties.[14] The secretariat, for its part, produced two basic documents that greatly helped shape the work of the ad hoc open-ended working group.[15]

Some of the principal discussions, which consumed many hours of negotiations, evolved around opposing views surrounding four main issues. The first was the jurisdictional dispute regarding "who does what" within the broader United Nations System. The Bretton Woods Institutions and their intergovernmental expressions—the board of governors and the executive boards—received their instructions from ministries of finance and central banks while the United Nations fell under the jurisdiction of ministries of foreign affairs. The well-known cleavage that persists in most countries among these different cabinet portfolios at the domestic level was reflected at the international level as well. There were even perceived ideological differences, with a prevailing view at the United Nations that the international financial institutions (IFIS) were more orthodox or conservative in economic policy matters, in contrast to a more liberal and progressive United Nations. There also was mutual suspicion among delegations and staff, based, among other matters, on the perception at the Bank and the Fund that the United Nations pursued encroaching on the mandates of the Bretton Woods Institutions, while, at the United Nations, some delegations (a minority) argued that the United Nations should, indeed, become the center of multilateralism in all areas, including finance.

The second issue revolved around "who does what" at the national level *vis à vis* the role of international cooperation. The long-held mindset of low and middle income countries, only slightly mitigated by the 1990s, was that in the sphere of international economic relations, the dice were loaded against them, and in favor of the high income countries.[16] Thus, in partial compensation for this handicap, in addition to the self-interest for donor countries in an expanding international economy, it had been argued that a target should be set for official development cooperation—it was labeled "foreign aid" at the time—that would enable the developing countries to achieve acceptable rates of growth.[17] In the 1970s, various proposals came forth arguing that the "economically advanced countries" should assign 0.7 percent of their gross national income to this purpose.[18] In fact, the International Development Strategy for the Second United Nations Development Decade indicated that "each economically advanced country should endeavor to provide by 1972 annually to developing countries financial resource transfers of a minimum net amount of 1 percent of its gross national product at market prices ..."[19] This issue, as well as the issue discussed in the previous paragraph, had a marked North-South cleavage to them, with the G77 insisting on the need of higher levels of international cooperation (with low conditionality and with the recipient country "in the driver's seat" in priority-setting) and the economically advanced countries demanding that low and middle income countries should get their own houses in order and refrain from using international assistance as a palliative for taking difficult domestic decisions, especially in the fiscal area.

The third issue in the discussions revolved around the age-old debate regarding the role of the state and the role of the market, and how these should interact in different societies. The tone of the discussion had become more subdued compared to the 1970s and most low and middle income countries had accepted a greater role for the market in the allocation of resources. Still, some economically advanced countries championed free market principles espoused in the "Washington Consensus",[20] while many low and middle income countries argued in favor of strong state leadership in promoting development. The common ground was that successful development experiences had generally found creative combinations of state and market, which usually reflected the historical, cultural, and economic peculiarities of each situation.

The fourth issue was related to the content and scope of the subject matter to be covered by the conference, with low and middle income countries arguing for a holistic approach and a wide ranging agenda, and most economically advanced countries favoring a more focused and selective agenda, heavily weighted on commitments to promote development. One of the items that became particularly contentious was the link between finance and trade, with the G77 insisting on including trade in the discussion; a notion that was at first resisted by developed countries. It should be recalled that at the time of the discussions the Uruguay Round (the 8th round of multilateral trade negotiations) had not yet come fully into effect, and countries were already preparing for the next round—the "Development Round"—which was launched in Doha, Qatar in November 2001. Another equally contentious issue referred to debt relief, or the debt overhang that became a major concern in the early 1980s, with aftereffects that were still present at the end of the 1990s.

Those main issues, and many additional areas of contention, were the subject of formulations in draft text, with language that was gradually ironed out in the series of formal and informal events carried out between February and the end of May 1999, with Mr. Libran Cabactulan, minister of the permanent mission of the Republic of the Philippines, acting as facilitator. The negotiations that took place also became a training ground for many of the experts that subsequently played a leading role in the preparatory process of the conference. Among them: Mauricio Escanero (Mexico), who would become the facilitator of the so-called finance for development (FfD) process; Ruth Jacoby (Sweden), an economist and former executive director in the

World Bank, who would become a co-chair of that process; Hacem Fahmy (Egypt), also destined to become a co-chair; Eduardo Gálvez (Chile); Sonia Leonce (Saint Lucia); Kwabena Osei-Danquah (Ghana); Andrés Franco (Colombia); Mubarak Hussein Rahmalla (Sudan); Navid Hanif (Pakistan); and Michael Gallagher as well as John Davidson (USA). The working group presented a complete report of its activities, with concrete recommendations and a decision to transmit same to the General Assembly for its consideration and appropriate action during the 54th session.[21]

The spirit in which the Working Group carried out its mandate is well captured in paragraph 20 of its report, when it says:

> we have an opportunity to begin the new millennium with a historic and goal-oriented collective political gesture of global solidarity for development and practical commitment to achieving it. To be successful, however, the momentum that is building at the United Nations will have to be nurtured and made to include all our prospective partners. An inclusive and continuing preparatory process will increase awareness and build international support and participation while it deepens the substance of the final event.[22]

The report also proposed as a conceptual framework the need to address "national, international and systemic issues relating to financing for development in a holistic manner in the context of globalization and interdependence." The working group went on to propose the scope of the event, an agenda, its form, and the modalities of the preparatory process.

The third phase

The preparatory process

On December 22 1999, the General Assembly adopted Resolution 54/196, which marked an important turning-point.[23] Not only did it endorse the report of the ad hoc open-ended working group in all its aspects (operative paragraph 1), but it took the final step in deciding to "convene in 2001 a high-level intergovernmental event of political decision makers, at least at the ministerial level, on financing for development, in the context of paragraph 20 of the report of the working group" (operative paragraph 2).

Further, the General Assembly decided to establish an intergovernmental preparatory committee, open to all states, to carry out the substantive preparations for the high-level intergovernmental event (operative paragraph 5) and took the highly unusual step to "constitute a Bureau of the Preparatory Committee, which will consist of fifteen representatives of Member States to the United Nations" (operative paragraph 8). What made it highly unusual was that almost all General Assembly committees or working groups have bureaus made up of five members (one for each of the regional groups). The fact that three members from each group had to be accommodated in this expanded bureau is an indication of the interest of member states to play a leading role in the proceedings. So many delegations wanted to be on the bureau that instead of weaning candidates down to the allotted number of posts, the number of posts was expanded. This decision had some consequences which are discussed below.

The resolution further embraced specific recommendations of the working group, including the broad participation of "all relevant stakeholders," and requested the Secretary-General to continue to support this initiative. Thus, resolution 54/196 marks the culmination of one process, led by the "Ad Hoc open ended Working Group," and the beginning of the next phase: the establishment of a preparatory committee, open to all states, and led by a bureau made up of fifteen members. The author was elected as one of the three persons belonging to the Latin American and Caribbean Group (Daúl Matute of Peru and Julian Hunte of Saint Lucia were the others).[24]

The transition from the working group to the preparatory committee should be viewed somewhat tantamount to a relay race. Much of the groundwork on form and substance had been developed by the working group, although at a fairly general level, with considerable inputs offered by the secretariat (especially the previously cited reports A/53/470 and A/53/479). Also, many of the main personalities involved in the preparatory committee, including the author, were the same that had participated in the working group. This not only gave the effort the continuity that facilitated the process of codifying the recommendations into what eventually ended up as the text known as the Monterrey Consensus, but also came accompanied by a collegiate atmosphere developed during the previous phase, which generated an environment conducive to reaching agreements on form and substance. The Secretary-General complied with General Assembly resolution 54/196 by providing "the Preparatory Committee and the high-level intergovernmental event with a secretariat commensurate with the level of the event and adequate staff ..."[25] The coordinating secretariat was headed by Oscar de Rojas, an experienced former diplomat from Venezuela, and it was assigned a small staff.[26]

The Secretary-General also provided his own orientations to the Preparatory Committee in a new report.[27]

Participating in the bureau of the preparatory committee during its two-year life span proved to be an engrossing and productive experience. The author still recalls the whole process as coming close to his own ideal of what the United Nations does best at the intergovernmental level, in developing an idea into specific and widely accepted proposals. What struck him especially were the content, tone, and level of the substantive discussions over the two-year period; a matter which moved the co-chairs to observe in a statement released on 8 May 2001 that the debate had been "a rich feast of substantive discussion."[28] In fact, in the same statement the co-chairs, when reviewing the preceding discussions since 1998, indicated the following:

> The financing for development process has been a unique inter-governmental exercise at the United Nations and as your Co-Chairs we believe that we have been fortunate to be a part of it. It began more than three years ago with an agreement in the General Assembly to do something important about a crucial issue. Exactly what would be done and exactly what the issue would encompass was purposefully left vague. Since then, we have added increasing precision to the process and the content as political support for the process evolved. We have discovered new ways to bring different parts of the international community together at the United Nations to jointly deliberate on crucial problems of mutual concern. Under the umbrella of the International Conference, we have become a coherent assemblage—one that is still evolving—of Governments and international institutions, with significant support from civil society organizations and, increasingly, from the business sector. Taking a holistic and integrated approach in its discussions, this assemblage has identified numerous policy needs in the area of financing of development. Henceforth, it will have to focus on which policy needs to address at the time that the International Conference begins in Monterrey, next March, and on how to address them.[29]

This long quotation is included because it reflects the author's own views regarding the careful and progressive consensus-building that took place, on both process and substance. Indeed, the preparatory process covered all the aspects one would wish to see leading to a major international conference. First, there was a conceptual framework, an agenda for action, policy orientations, and partnering with other stakeholders (in this particular case, the Bretton Woods Institutions and other international financial institutions). Second, a broad alliance was developed with non-governmental institutions, academia, the private sector, parliamentarians, and, in general, civil society. Third, a much broader participation of different national portfolios was present in official delegations, especially from ministries of finance and trade. Fourth, as was the case with the Millennium Summit, the preparatory process for the Monterrey conference also counted with strong leadership (on the part of the co-chairs, the bureau, and the facilitator). As mentioned in their previously cited statement, the co-chairs were able to foster a favorable environment which helped to overcome the usual North-South cleavage, in spite of highly contentious issues which were the object of spirited debates through the final revisions of the draft declaration. Still another important ingredient was the substantive support received from the secretariat.

A final and crucial element for the successful preparatory process was the unusually active and constructive role on the part of the host government of the event, even before it formalized its offer of a venue in mid-2001. Moreover, one of the most frustrating aspects of multilateral diplomacy—the ritual it involves, the lengthy debates—turned out in this particular case to become an asset, as issues and policy differences were worked out and ideas were matured through what became a cumulative and progressive exercise, instilling a sense of ownership in most of the delegates participating in same.

The work of the preparatory committee

The preparatory committee held an organizational session, and four formal sessions, although each one of those involved numerous meetings, and sometimes resumed sessions, as well as many informal consultations.[30] To those that participated in this activity, it felt as a virtually permanent session during almost two years (2000–2001); this was especially the case for the 15 members of the Bureau, which met frequently, added to the obligation of a number of them to be present at some of the regional consultations—the five regional commissions organized consultations on their respective regions' perspective on financing for development between August and December 2001—and the hearings with NGOs and the private sector. The committee was also informed by the contents of the Zedillo Panel's Report which had been commissioned previously by the Secretary-General.[31]

Although a sense of camaraderie was developed between the members of the preparatory committee (during the two-year period, in about half the cases the originally designated persons continued their assignments to the end of the Conference), the interaction among them predictably went beyond the normal functions of a Bureau, which tend to be mostly of a procedural nature. In this specific instance, a body of 15 members, with three each for the main regional groups, tended to take on an element of negotiation (or pre-negotiation) on both procedural and substantive matters. In balance, the different points of view that prevailed within the bureau made work more, rather than less, difficult, and confirmed the author's personal conviction that it is preferable to maintain the practice of bureaus made up of five persons, and limited to procedural activities. On the other hand, the successful role of a single facilitator in this specific instance also confirmed the author's personal conviction that one facilitator is preferable to two, as has been the prevailing practice in recent years (the need for the two facilitators to project a common front sometimes involves a bit of negotiation between them).

This is not the place to recall the details of each of the meetings held by the preparatory committee, nor the issues raised and how they were resolved. Much of the information is contained in the reports prepared after every session.[32] Nor is it necessary to offer a chronology of events, since this information is easily available to the reader.[33] Although the organizational sessions' agenda was focused on process—exploring modalities of participation of non-UN stakeholders, in the preparatory process and in the conference itself—in subsequent meetings both process and substance were addressed simultaneously, especially beginning with the second session of February 2001, and even more so the third session of May 2001, which already had at its disposal a first working paper prepared by the Facilitator, who ably distilled the progress achieved in previous substantive debates on the main issue areas that had been identified.[34] The results of this renewed and much more focused debate permitted the facilitator to prepare his first draft outcome document, which was considered by the preparatory committee at its renewed third session in October.

The final and most crucial meeting of the preparatory committee was held in New York from 14–27 January 2002, followed by a one-day meeting on 15 February to adopt the draft text of the Monterrey Consensus, whose contents had been agreed upon at informal consultations on 27 January 2002.[35] The author's overall recollection of the final days of the meetings is that they became extremely tense around very few but very controversial issues. What stuck in the author's mind, more than the specific nature of the paragraphs in contention, is the image of the long days and nights—including an "all-nighter"—spent in the basement of the United Nations Head-quarters trying to resolve the matters in dispute. Part of the discussion was the usual last-minute posturing on the part of different delegations, but the other part was reflected in opposing positions regarding the links between domestic policies and international cooperation. This pitted the spokesperson of the G77 and a few of his delegates against the representative of the United States, joined occasionally by the spokesperson of the European Union. Ultimately, those differences were ironed out, and white smoke emerged at dawn on January 27. The facilitator, Mauricio Escanedo, had played an exemplary role, as had Ruth Jacoby in her double role as co-chair and DPR of the Mission of Sweden, supported by her other co-chair Hazem Fahmy.[36]

The Monterrey Conference

The successful preparatory process was of course instrumental in the equally successful outcome of the Conference, held in Monterrey, Mexico, from 18–22 March 2002. In fact, the latter turned out to be one of the more memorable events in the long list of summits orga-nized by the United Nations that the author had attended in the pre-vious decade. It brought together over 50 heads of state and government, foreign ministers, finance ministers, senior executives of international organizations and private multinational firms, distinguished personalities, and non-governmental organizations. The conference included the customary plenary sessions, at the level of senior officials, then ministers, and, finally, heads of state. There also was a special retreat for an informal dialogue to which only heads of state were invited by President Vicente Fox of Mexico.[37] Four Summit round tables were held, each dedicated to a different topic, complemented by 16 multi-stakeholder round tables. Three forums—one each of non-governmental organizations, international business executives, and parliamentarians—were also held.[38] This considerable mobilization of delegates and personalities was complemented by numerous side-events (not all of them satisfied with the outcome of the conference).[39]

The conference also had its anecdotal moments. Thanks to intense lobbying efforts on the part of the Mexican Government, both Pre-sident George W. Bush of the United States and President Fidel Castro of Cuba agreed to participate in the event. Much planning must have gone into assuring that the paths of both dignitaries would not cross at any time. This goal was successfully achieved.

But what made the event most meaningful was its principal out-come, the Monterrey Consensus, which reflected all the inputs of the preparatory process and even the preceding working group.[40] By UN standards it was short (74 paragraphs), coherent, eminently implementable, and with the potential to have tangible impact on development issues. Rather than stressing the North-South division, the Consensus pursued a partnership, where "each country has primary responsibility for its own economic and social development", while, "at the same time, domestic economies are now interwoven with the global economic system and, inter alia, the effective use of trade and investment opportunities can help countries to fight poverty."[41]

The essence of the message was that the developing world would do its share, but it also needed support from the more advanced countries and an enabling international economic environment. This partnership was proposed in the spirit of "achieving the internationally agreed development goals, including those contained in the Millennium Declaration."[42] The main weakness in the Consensus document is related to the follow-up arrangements. The provisions appear in chapter III ("Staying engaged") and especially in paragraph 69, which is rather fuzzy in distributing responsibilities between the General Assembly and the Economic and Social Council on follow-up matters, leaving the sensation that none of the principal organs was clearly in charge.

But returning to the positive aspects, while it is hard to draw a cause-and-effect relationship between the Monterrey Consensus and its impact on Official Development Assistance (ODA), it is noteworthy that the level of ODA, which had been declining in previous years, reached a turning point in 2002, and increased significantly in subsequent years, at least prior to the 2008 financial crisis. Measuring net ODA as a percentage of gross national income, this was true of most OECD members, and particularly of the United States.[43] In fact, the latter country established a new and independent foreign assistance agency, the Millennium Challenge Account, whose outlines were already announced by President Bush at the Monterrey Conference, and which came into being in 2004.[44] In addition to the outcome document, the Conference was a gigantic and successful public awareness initiative, meant to impact on priority setting and policy implementation at the national and international levels. It also led to two major follow-up events: one in Doha in November 2008 and the other in Addis Ababa in July 2015.[45]

Conclusion

What were the main "take-aways" of this protracted negotiation? First, a confirmation that multilateral diplomacy at the United Nations usually works at a very slow pace, given the need to build consensus among 188 parties (the total membership at the time). Logically, the more contentious the issues, the longer it takes to find a meeting of the minds among member states. But it also showed that persistence seemed to pay off. Indeed, what initially appeared to be intractable differences gradually gave way to accommodations built on compromises. It took time, but in the end produced results.

A second factor that had helped in moving the process forward was the very active engagement and advocacy role of non-state actors, including academics, NGOs, and representatives of the business sector. This was an important finding, given the resistance shown by some delegations to "outsider" participation, under the premise that the United Nations was an organization made up only of member states. Most non-state actors were favorable to holding a conference on financing for development, and thus contributed to mitigating the original opposition of some of the advanced economies. They, as well as parliamentarians, also played an important role in the actual shaping and finally holding of the Conference.

Third, perhaps for the first time since the post-war period, the different multilateral institutions that were set up as the anchors of the post-war order—the United Nations, the Bretton Woods Institutions, and the unrealized International Trade Organization, downgraded to the General Agreement on Trade and Tariffs (and, since 1995, converted into the World Trade Organization)—seemed to be poised to productively engage on matters of common interest. Admittedly, it was modest progress, given the profound differences that had developed over the years among these institutions due to dissimilar world views, different governance structures, and diverse purposes. But modest progress was achieved in contrast to the generally contentious relationship that had characterized prior relations between the United Nations and the Bretton Woods Institutions.[46]

Having these institutions work together for the good of their common membership, while at the same time respecting the above-mentioned differences, was spelled out as an aspiration in 1993 when the General Assembly expressed the desire to "enhance the role of the United Nations and the relationship between the United Nations and the Bretton Woods institutions in the promotion of international cooperation for development, within the framework and provision of the Charter of the United Nations and the Articles of Agreement of the Bretton Woods Institutions ..."[47] The aspiration of 1993 seems only to have assumed real substance nine years later at Monterrey.

Fourth, the fact that the Conference was held away from United Nations Headquarters turned out to be an important benefit. As already pointed out, among its other characteristics it gave the host government a privileged status in the negotiations and the actual organization of the conference. As already mentioned, a delegate from Mexico played a crucial role as facilitator of the preparatory process: much of the final text, both in structure and content, flowed from his hard work and patience in accommodating different stakeholders' comments to the evolving draft. The Mexican government, all the way from President Vicente Fox and his permanent representative to the United Nations,[48] down to the large amount of officials involved, not only offered an impeccable venue, but played a decisive role in assuring the presence of numerous heads of state. Undoubtedly, some of these felt more swayed to participate due to the bilateral representations made to them by Mexico than by the desire to partake in yet one more international conference, but at any rate they were present in Monterrey.

Fifth, as already mentioned, the preparatory process was one of the rare instances in which the United Nations was able to convene a broad array of delegates from member states, normally represented mostly by ministries of foreign affairs. On this occasion, there was also an important presence of ministries of finance, trade, cooperation, and even central banks. They were involved not only in the final conference, but also in the preparatory process. For its part, the secretariat had multiple areas of its staff engaged, including the Department of Economic and Social Affairs, the United Nations Conference on Trade and Development, and the regional commissions, in addition to various funds and programs.

All in all, then, from the author's perspective, in a span of two years the United Nations had brought off two major international conferences with superior outputs: the Millennium Summit in New York, and the Financing for Development Conference in Monterrey, Mexico. Both events have to be regarded as successful products of multilateral diplomacy, and both events benefitted from several crucial characteristics that made a difference.

In fact, there are some parallelisms between the Millennium Summit and the International Conference, but even more differences. In the latter case, the negotiations were much more contentious and the involvement of the secretariat somewhat less. In addition, there were three important features that distinguish this event from the 2000 Summit. First, an unusual system of governance was devised for the preparatory process, by creating a preparatory committee with a bureau of 15 members. Second, it was held away from United Nations headquarters.

And, third, non-governmental actors played an even more active role than in previous conferences, especially during the preparatory process. But, again in both instances, all the complicated pieces of the puzzle came together in both of these historic events.

Notes

1 General Assembly resolution 55/2, 8 September 2000, op. 14.
2 General Assembly resolution 45/199, 21 December 1990.
3 General Assembly resolution S-18/3, 1 May 1990.
4 General Assembly decision 1991/274, 26 July 1991.
5 General Assembly resolution 46/205, 20 December 1991.
6 General Assembly decision 47/436, 18 December 1992.
7 General Assembly resolution 48/187, 21 December 1993, op. 1 and 3.
8 General Assembly resolution 50/93, 20 December 1995.
9 General Assembly resolution 52/179, 18 December 1997, op. 4.
10 General Assembly resolution 52/179, 18 December 1997, op. 6 and 7.
11 General Assembly resolution 53/173, 15 December 1998.
12 From the author's personal perspective, the decisions mentioned in the previous paragraph and the beginning of the preparatory work could not have come at a more opportune time. Opportune, because the author had barely taken up his duties in New York six weeks earlier, and was trying to position his delegation in an area of expertise where a relatively small country could make a contribution. Given his own background, at home and at the Economic Commission for Latin America and the Caribbean (ECLAC), finance for development looked like a perfect match. It turned out to be a full immersion in multilateral diplomacy at the United Nations, and facilitated networking with some of the key players.
13 For a fuller accounting of the work of the Committee, see: *Report of the Ad Hoc Open Working Group of the General Assembly on Financing for Development, Supplement No. 28* (A/54/28), United Nations, New York 1999.
14 See: www.un.org/esa/ffd, the successor site for www.un.org/esa/analysis/ffd
15 See: *High-level international intergovernmental consideration of financing for development: recurring themes and key elements: Note by the Secretary-General* (A/53/470) 8 October 1998; and *High-level international intergovernmental consideration of financing for development: work of the United Nations system, Report of the Secretary-General* (A/53/479) 9 October 1998.
16 The Economic Commission for Latin America and the Caribbean had done much in its pioneering years to propagate the theory that argued, in its most simplified version, that in the long run the evolution of the terms of trade punished producers of primary products and favored producers of industrialized goods. Thus a conceptual framework was set up that favored industrialization, as well as the "North-South" cleavage that informed much of the work of the United Nations at the time, and still has adherents up to the present.
17 Some of the pioneering work on this matter was undertaken by Jan Tinbergen, in his capacity as Chairman of the United Nations Committee on Development Planning. See: *DAC Journal 2002* (Vol 3 No 4) III-9–III-11.

18 The best known proposal was made by the Commission chaired by Lester Pearson in the Report entitled *Partners in Development* (London: Pall Mall Press, 1969).

19 General Assembly resolution 2626 (XXV), 24 October 1970, op. 42.

20 The term coined by John Williamson of the Institute for International Economics in 1989 for a standard set of mostly market-led policy prescriptions.

21 *Report of the Ad Hoc Open Working Group of the General Assembly on Financing for Development Supplement No. 28* (A/54/28), United Nations, New York, 1999.

22 Ibid., paragraphs 17–19.

23 The Economic and Social Council also welcomed the broad agreement reached in the context of the Ad Hoc Open-ended Working Group in its resolution 1999/51. See: *Report of the Economic and Social Council for 1999* (A/54/3/Rev.1), 2.

24 Julian Hunte was the Permanent Representative of Saint Lucia and subsequently was elected as President of the 58th session of the General Assembly. He was replaced in the Bureau by Sonia Leonce in the course of the Preparatory Committee's work. Likewise, Daúl Matute was replaced by Jorge Valdéz. A full list of the officers elected to the bureau during the first organizational session of the Preparatory Committee can be found in Report A/55/28, page 1.

25 General Assembly resolution 54/196, op. 17.

26 Alexander Trepelkov, Harris Glekman, Krishnan Sharma, Federica Pietracci and Marcela Guimaraes.

27 *Report of the Secretary-General to the Preparatory Committee*, (A/AC.257/12), 18 December 2000.

28 *Report of the Preparatory Committee for the High-level International Intergovernmental Event on Financing for Development, Supplement No. 28 B* (A/55/28/Add.2), Annex 7.

29 Ibid., 7.

30 The organizational and resumed organizational sessions were held on 10 and 25 February, 27, 28 and 31 March and 30 May 2000; the first session was held on 31 May and 2 June 2000, and the resumed first session on 30 October and on 16, 20 and 27 November 2000; the second session was held from 12 to 23 February 2001; the third session was held from 2 to 8 May 2004, the resumed third session was held from 15 to 19 October 2001; and the fourth session was held from 14 to 25 January, 2002. All meetings were held in New York. Most had at least five meetings plus numerous informal consultations. Their recommendations were approved by the General Assembly in resolutions 55/245A, 21 March 2001; 55/245B, 25 July 2001, and 55/213, 20 December 2000.

31 The Secretary-General appointed a panel of 11 experts in December 2000, headed by Ernesto Zedillo, ex-President of Mexico, to propose measures to address the financial needs of the world's developing countries. The Panel's Report was submitted as A/55/1000 of 26 June 2001.

32 The Reports of the Bureau on the Preparatory Committee's five sessions can be found in: A/AC.257/6, 23 March 2000; A/AC.257/8, 25 May 2000; A/AC.257/22, 15 April 2001; A/AC.257/29, 10 October 2001 and A/AC.257/33, 2 January 2002.

33 For a fairly complete chronology of events, see: www.un.org/esa/ffd/over view/chronology

34 A/AC.257/22, 22 April 2001.

35 A/AC.257/32, 7 December 2001.

36 The original co-chairs were Jorgen Bójer (Denmark) and Asda Jayanama (Thailand), but the bulk of the substantive work in 2001 occurred after both had transferred their responsibilities to Ruth Jacoby and Hazem Fahmy.

37 See: A/56/920, 18 April 2002.

38 See: *Final Plenary Communique by the Business Interlocutors to the UN Conference on Financing for Development* (Monterrey, 22 March 2002); as well as summaries of multi-stakeholder round tables, all on: www.un.org/esa/ffd/overview/chronology

39 For example, the Global Forum on Financing the Right to Equitable and Sustainable Development issued the following declaration on 16 March 2002: "The Monterrey Consensus offers no mechanisms to mobilize new financial resources to achieve the Millennium Development Goals. For this reason, the organizations participating in the Global Forum ... are NOT part of the Monterrey Consensus. The participating organizations of the Global Forum would like to share the declaration which resulted from three days of intense work and participation by 2600 persons, 700 General Assembly organizations and 80 countries from all the regions of the world. Our Monterrey Declaration is a review of the General Assembly's negative economic, social, environmental gender and cultural impacts of the current neo-liberal policies. These policies are repeated in the Monterrey 'consensus.' Our Monterrey Declaration is a statement of the visions and proposals for policies, which would serve humanity and the environment in which we live."

40 *Monterrey Consensus* (A/CONF.198/11), endorsed by the General Assembly on 9 July 2002 through resolution 56/210.

41 Paragraph 6 of the Monterrey Consensus.

42 Paragraph 4 of the Monterrey Consensus.

43 DAC https://data.oecd.org/oda/net-oda.htm

44 At the Summit, President Bush said the following in his remarks: "I have proposed a 50-percent increase in our core development assistance over the next three budget years. Eventually, this will mean a $5 billion annual increase over current levels. These new funds will go into a new Millennium Challenge Account, devoted to projects in nations that govern justly, invest in their people and encourage economic freedom." Also see: www.mcc.gov/

45 See: "Doha Declaration on Financing for Development" 2 December 2008, endorsed by the General Assembly in its resolution 63/239, 24 December 2008, and *Addis Ababa Action Agenda of the Third International Conference on Financing for Development* of 16 July 2015; endorsed by the General Assembly on 27 July 2015 through resolution 69/313.

46 ECOSOC has been holding up to 2015 a yearly one-day meeting with the Bretton Woods Institutions since 1998 (see Chapter 4). Still, profound differences persist to this day among the United Nations and the BW Institutions in their bureaucratic cultures, their system of governance, the way their respective staffs perceive each other, and their treaty-established purposes.

47 General Assembly resolution 47/181, 17 March 1993. The matter of relations between the UN and the Bretton Woods Institutions has a long history, and was addressed formally on a yearly basis by the General Assembly. See, for example: resolutions 50/227, 24 February 1996 and resolution 51/166, 16 December 1996.
48 First Manuel Tello Macias, and, in 2001, Jorge Eduardo Navarrete.

3 The 2000–2001 battle over the scale of assessments in the Fifth Committee[1]

- **The opening shot**
- **Dynamics of the negotiation in the fifth committee**
- **The foundations of an agreement**
- **The final decisive stage**
- **An assessment of the outcome**
- **Conclusion**

On Saturday 23 December 2000, when most United Nations delegates had left for the Christmas break, the General Assembly approved the new scales of assessment for the United Nations' regular budget as well as for the budget of its peacekeeping operations. Thus ended an extended, complex, and sometimes even dramatic negotiation, which certainly deserves a place in the annals of multilateral diplomacy at the United Nations. It is a story of high political profile, as well as an illustration of how the main committees of the General Assembly carry on their work. The author was able to follow the process as a privileged participant, in his capacity as president of the General Assembly's fifth committee (on administrative and budgetary matters). It also marked one of the few, if not the only moments in history when the business of the fifth committee, usually of a highly technical nature, was diligently followed by the permanent representatives.

The immediate precedent for this exceptional flurry of interest can be found in the Helms-Biden legislation, adopted by the United States Senate in June 1999 and enacted by Congress in November of that year.[2] Under the overall objective of "reforming" the United Nations, the legislation set certain conditions for the payment of part of the United States' arrears to the United Nations. Those conditions included a reduction of the US contribution to the regular budget, from 25 percent to 22 percent, and to peacekeeping operations, from around 31 percent to 25 percent.[3]

These conditions were widely condemned by the rest of the international community as illegal, unilateral, unfair, and arbitrary. Illegal, because the US, as any other member state, is obligated to meet its commitments to the UN budget in full, on time, and without conditions. Unilateral, because the legislative branch of a member state mandated its executive branch to act, committing it to present its position on a "take it or leave it" basis, rather than reaching an agreement as a result of consultations and negotiations, compatible with decision-making in a multilateral organization. Unfair, because in accordance with the long-established principle of capacity to pay, the US contribution of 25 percent to the regular budget was, in fact, already below the country's relative participation in global GNP. And arbitrary, because the 22 percent threshold had no logical basis; it could equally have been any other coefficient.

The mood at the UN was one of outrage, pitting virtually all delegations—of developed and developing countries—against the United States. And, of course, there was a mixture of apprehension and curiosity regarding how this clash between 187 states on the one side against one state on the other would finally play out.

The opening shot

The United States administration launched a singularly aggressive and comprehensive campaign in order to be able to comply with the Helms-Biden legislation, arguing that, from the vantage point of its domestic political landscape, it was the only way to be able to pay its considerable arrears (almost 1 billion dollars) and rebuild its standing at the United Nations. While mindful of the strong resistance and even resentment that the legislation induced in most quarters outside of the US, the latter's official policy held that compliance with the legislation was in the best interests of the United Nations, since it would put the US–UN relations on a new, improved, and stable footing. In fact, compliance with Helms-Biden became a major objective of US foreign policy.[4]

Strong *démarches* were made in virtually every capital, letters were written by the Secretary of State to his counterparts, while the permanent representative of the United States to the United Nations, Richard Holbrooke, traveled around the world to press the case to other member states. The bilateral relation between the US and any particular country was invoked in requesting support for the US position. And many middle-income governments were pressed to voluntarily raise their contributions to the UN budgets (regular and especially peacekeeping) to make up for the short-fall that the decline in US contributions would inevitably generate in what was essentially a zero-sum game (i.e., to the degree that the United States lowered the proportion of its contributions to the UN budget, others would have to pick up the slack). Finally, a strong team was assembled at the US mission, including a seasoned career diplomat, Donald Hays, to head the day-to-day negotiations, and a professional "numbers cruncher," Suzanne Nossel, at that time drafted from the private sector. Moreover, after the US converted the issue into a high-stakes affair, other member states followed suit.[5]

Dynamics of the negotiation in the fifth committee

The agenda items on the scale of assessments were introduced in the fifth committee on 2–6 October (regular budget, agenda item 122) and 3–6 October (peacekeeping, agenda item 169). In what was a highly atypical circumstance in the fifth committee, numerous ambassadors were in attendance, responding not only to the prodding of Richard Holbrooke (he had written a letter to all his colleagues urging their presence) but also due to the high profile that the topic had acquired by then. Initial reactions to at least one of the US proposals—to lower the ceiling on the regular budget scale—were not at all encouraging. Delegation after delegation rejected such a move, arguing, among other aspects, that it went against the principle of capacity to pay.

However, upon closer examination of the statements (most of their texts were distributed), the rejection was couched in careful language, suggesting that many of the governments had already succumbed, partially or totally, to bilateral US initiatives. Indeed, many of the smaller countries had been "persuaded" that the matter did not concern them, since under any scenario their contribution to the UN regular budget in nominal terms would barely be affected by the change in the scale of assessments. The argument was sugar-coated in several cases with some modest concessions on bilateral issues. While none of these countries would openly support the US position, their opposition as expressed in the meeting hall was quite muted. It was up to the larger contributors to the UN budget to pick up the slack left if the US relative contribution diminished, and most of these strenuously rejected this possibility.

When the matter of simultaneously updating the scale of assessments to finance the peace-keeping budget came up, in the belief that some trade-offs could be fashioned by addressing overall budgetary commitments to the UN, the European Union reacted with great enthusiasm, but most developing countries emphatically did not. Rather, many suggested de-coupling the discussion of both scales of assessment, and proposed that this second item could wait until the resumed session of March 2001.

Subsequently, as is the custom, both items were relegated to informal consultations; Movses Abelian of Armenia was designated the facilitator on the scale of assessments for peacekeeping and Frank Smyth of Ireland the facilitator of the scale of assessments for the regular budget. Between the end of October and 8 December, 15 sessions were held on the scale of assessments of the regular budget, and 11 on the scale of assessment of the peacekeeping budget. However, very little, if any, progress was achieved. Both coordinators were getting increasingly frustrated and called for a smaller working-group, as well as the active intervention of the permanent representatives. The author's own impression from attending some of these "informals" was that there was no desire nor will to move ahead. On the other hand, it was well known that the slow pace of negotiations was a deep-rooted part of the bureaucratic culture of the fifth committee, and that when faced with difficult decisions, delegates tended to procrastinate. That is why in the past most deals had been struck in the final hours of the session, with the Christmas break as the unmovable deadline.[6]

More specifically, several reasons can be cited for the lack of progress. First, there was a culture of micro management in the fifth committee (it persists to the present), so at least some of the delegations tended to scrutinize matters exhaustively. Second, since the mid-1980s, agreements in the committee were taken by consensus, which naturally made all decision-making slow and arduous. Third, this particular issue was perceived by many as an imposition on the part of the main contributor to the UN budget (as indeed it was), igniting strong feelings of rejection. And, finally, the intellectual case for lowering the ceiling in the methodology of the scale for the regular budget was actually quite weak. Rather, if capacity to pay were to be the principal criteria, the US contribution should, if anything, have been raised, and not lowered, given that country's participation in global GNP, which at that time surpassed 27 percent. Possibly a political case could have been made for lowering the ceiling (insuring the long-term commitments of the main contributor to the UN budget, even if it meant a somewhat reduced contribution), but this broader perspective was in the purview of permanent representatives, and not relevant for their specialists assigned to the fifth committee.

From the author's frequent conversations with Richard Holbrooke, the general outline of the latter's arguments can be summarized as follows. First, for other potential major contributors to the UN budget, many of them were way below the "capacity to pay" criteria. Among the "targeted" countries: China, the Russian Federation, the Gulf States (oil producers), the Republic of Korea, Singapore, India, and other South-Asian economies that had performed well in the past years. Second, to the vast majority of developing countries, whatever the outcome of the negotiation it would not affect them in a significant way in nominal terms; to bolster the argument, an increase in the gradient (discount for developing countries) was proposed. Third, but not very convincingly, the lowering of the ceiling would be beneficial for the UN since it would reduce the relative influence of the United States in overall decision-making in a multilateral organization where all countries were considered equal. Fourth and most importantly, the integrity of the UN budget was at stake, since not complying with the Helms-Biden legislation put future US contributions to both the regular and peacekeeping budgets of the UN at serious risk. The first three arguments were "carrots"; the last can be considered a "stick."

On 8 December, after much prodding by Ambassador Holbrooke and with deadlines looming ever closer, a decision was taken to introduce a new, higher-profile phase to the proceedings; or, as it were, to get into "high gear." On that day, a meeting of the fifth committee was convened at the level of ambassadors. This meeting had been carefully prepared through previous consultations with numerous delegates who understood what was at stake as well as the difficulties that lay in the way of reaching agreement on both scales of assessments. Although the positions expressed by delegations in the original 2–6 October session were restated in this new session, the language on not lowering the ceiling was now even more muted. It was apparent that the strong US *démarches* at the bilateral level were having an impact, especially in some of the smaller developing countries.

There was, however, some confusion regarding the path for moving forward. During several weeks, a division had developed within the fifth committee along a traditional cleavage on procedure. Some delegations favored establishing a small working group, under the understanding that it was a more agile way of advancing. Others felt that the matter was far too important to delegate it to a working group, and insisted on functioning in the format of the "Committee of the Whole." Finally, by 8 December, and over the stern objections of some delegations (who argued in favor of total transparency), the creation of a smaller, but open-ended working group was accepted. Ambassadors committed themselves to actively participate in the final weeks of deliberation, and the president was authorized to organize consultations with "friends of the chair." The meeting ended on a rather optimistic note, with the general impression that the committee would now, finally, get down to business.

After the meeting, the author was immediately approached by Richard Holbrooke and asked to convene a small meeting of permanent representatives, which included the US, the EU, Japan, and Australia. The author indicated to Ambassador Holbrooke that such a limited gathering could compromise his own role as president of the committee, and suggested that the US should take the initiative and try to iron out their differences with the EU and Japan in bilateral consultations before moving on to a "Friends of the Chair" session. Ambassador Holbrooke agreed, and thus a parallel avenue of consultations was initiated. Most of the informal gatherings of this group were held at the US mission at the Waldorf Astoria Towers. The president was kept abreast of these conversations both by the US and French ambassadors, but never participated in the same. While multilateral diplomacy requires the full participation of all parties, it seemed perfectly acceptable to seek short-cuts to reach a final consensus, especially with the ever decreasing time frame available. But it seemed equally important to preserve the president's impartiality.

The very limited informal consultations between the main contributors to the UN budget were gradually expanded to include other actors, and notably the Río Group, virtually unknown up to then in New York.[7] This Group had stumbled into a pro-active role on the matter almost by accident (and a little as a result of the author's prodding Alfonso Valdivieso, the permanent representative of Colombia, to take a more active role). Several of the individual members of the Rio Group had major interests at play. The Mexican mission had developed a creative proposal over the preceding months to establish different levels between the existing categories denominated A, B, C, and D of the peacekeeping budget, in order to graduate assessments in line with per capita income. Brazil faced a steep increase in its contribution to the regular budget, as did, to a lesser degree, Colombia, Chile, and Uruguay, while Argentina faced even more dramatic increases in its contributions to the peacekeeping budget.

As the number of participants in the informal consultations taking place at the US mission increased, the author's concerns grew apace, fearing a revolt of those delegations that demanded full transparency in the negotiations. These concerns were shared with Ambassador Holbrooke, who readily agreed to let Alfonso Valdivieso, in his capacity as Chair of the Rio Group, take a more pro-active role. This could include hosting the informal consultations at the Colombian mission, and expanding the list of participants to bring additional players aboard. Ambassador Valdivieso had already managed to forge a common position among the delegations of Chile, Mexico, Argentina, and Brazil, in spite of the opposing interests of Brazil (concerned with the regular budget) and Argentina (concerned with the peacekeeping budget). They all understood that supporting each other gave them leverage in the upcoming negotiations, and adopted as their own the Mexican proposal mentioned earlier to modify the scale of assessments for peacekeeping.

The venue of the consultations moved to the Colombian mission during the week-end of 16 and 17 December, and among the new delegations invited were Singapore, Korea, Egypt, South Africa, India, United Arab Emirates, Nigeria, and, belatedly, China. Some progress was made in designing the architecture of a scale for peacekeeping operations, and an outline was discussed (but not agreed upon) for the regular budget. While the author scrupulously avoided any participation in this initiative, Alfonso Valdivieso kept him permanently informed and asked for feedbacks.

Simultaneously, during the week of 11 December the "friends of the chair" working group met on a daily basis. Although it was conceived as a small working group, many delegations insisted it be open to all, so contrary to our expectations, these meetings were amply attended, and could not be carried out in a more intimate setting. Indeed, those meetings had to be moved to a larger hall in order to accommodate up to 150 delegates. Further, participants were basically fifth committee delegates, with only a sprinkling of ambassadors present. Again, there was a sensation that things were not moving, but now, in part, because delegates knew of the parallel talks going on in the mission of Colombia, and opted to await their outcome.

In order to inject some forward movement in the process, the author decided to table a document to frame the upcoming negotiations. It was described as a working paper, rather than a proposal, and had been prepared with the help of the secretariat. The document contained four sets of alternatives: a ceiling of 22 percent and another of 25 percent, and a gradient (as explained before, a "discount" granted to developing countries on what would have been their normal contribution under the "capacity to pay" criteria) of 80 percent and one of 75 percent, except for the category of Least Developed Countries (LDCs), which had a gradient of 85 percent.[8] The working paper provided the numerical limits of what each alternative meant for individual countries. It also had one innovative idea: a phasing-in period of three years for all countries that experienced a brusque increase in their contribution to the regular budget of 50 percent or more, in order to make such an increase a little more palatable. This phasing-in was to be financed by all countries that did not experience such an abrupt increase (this provoked some adverse reactions, since some low-income countries understandably objected to the notion of subsidizing the impact that higher-income countries were supposed to absorb).

The foundations of an agreement

Since specifics were involved, a larger number of ambassadors participated in the meeting on 14 December, and a fairly productive discussion ensued around the working paper. Five features emerged from the discussion, all of which were to shape what became the final scale of assessments. The first was the idea of some type of phasing-in for seriously affected countries, and especially developing countries. The second was the reaction that only developed countries or higher-income developing countries should be expected to finance the phasing-in. The third was the result of a reaction of Japan, which led to the shortening of the base period. Japan, in effect, made an impassioned plea that under no circumstance could its contribution to the regular budget exceed 20 percent (in the Chairman's proposal, that limit had been exceeded in the first year). Japan proposed changing the base period from six years (in the original proposal) to three years, which greatly helped Japan, given the relatively poor economic performance of the country in the immediately preceding years, and its declining participation in global GNP. Fourth, Japan also proposed a "sliding gradient", which contemplated differentiated gradients as a function of individual countries' economic characteristics. This idea was emphatically rejected by developing countries, and especially by China, which felt that it was conceived to increase its own contribution. However, this rejection tended to consolidate the idea that the gradient of 80 percent should be maintained. Finally, some delegations actually expressed resignation, if not support, to the idea that the ceiling could, indeed, come down to 22 percent. In short, the basic framework of an agreement appeared within reach at the end of the meeting.

Moreover, an even broader strategy appeared to be emerging. This consisted in using the different parameters that make up the scale of assessments—the "capacity to pay" based on participation in world GNP, the base period used (the average of from anywhere from three to six years), the "gradient" or adjustment for developing countries and LDCs, the debt burden adjustment, the basis for converting local currencies into comparable exchange rates, and others—to tailor a final scale which could accommodate the "red lines" that different important players brought to the table. Japan was not willing to pay more than 20 percent of the regular budget because its population allegedly would not stand for it? Let's devise a scale that meets that requirement by lowering the average of the base period. The Republic of Korea is not willing to absorb a dramatic increase in its contribution to the regular budget? Let's devise a gradual phasing-in that would make it more palatable, at least in the first year. Brazil feels that its own contribution to the regular budget is flagrantly disproportionate? Let's look at the underlying methodology for establishing the market exchange rate of Brazilian *reals* to dollars. This put rational criteria to work for what was an irrational outcome; something like putting the cart before the horse by identifying the limits of each major player and then designing the criteria to meet those limits. It should be pointed out that this approach was undertaken cautiously, with an eye to not distorting the integrity of a methodology that everyone could support.

Although some important parameters were thus identified, there was still some distance to go to reach the final phase of the process. On Friday 15 December, the President of the General Assembly decided to convene a small group of influential ambassadors to have a frank exchange of views as well as a discussion on how to move forward. Present were all of the main actors, including the permanent representatives of Argentina, Algeria, Australia, Bahamas, China, Colombia, Egypt, France, India, Iran, Morocco, Nepal, Nigeria, Norway, Philippines, Qatar, Republic of Korea, the Russian Federation, the United Arab Emirates, the United States, the United Kingdom, Singapore, and Sweden. A very frank discussion took place, to the point that there were some sharp exchanges, especially between Richard Holbrooke and Kishore Mahbubani of Singapore. However, the discussion had cleared the air somewhat, and had paved the way for a productive re-entry of the parallel discussions into the fifth committee.

During the weekend of 16 and 17 December, it became clear that the consultations in the Colombian mission had advanced significantly. As mentioned earlier, these centered on peacekeeping, but the regular budget scale was also discussed. At the same time, the secretariat prepared an alternative proposal for the scale of assessment of the regular budget which drew heavily on both the meeting of 14 December described above and the consultations that had taken place in the Colombian mission. This scale was based on average statistical base periods of four and a half years, a low per capita income adjustment of 80 percent, with the threshold per capita income limit of the global average per capita GNP, and a debt burden approach based on flows, except for heavily indebted poor countries (HIPC), which was based on stock.[9] It also incorporated a three-year phase-in for countries experiencing abrupt (55 percent or more) increases in their assessments, to be financed principally by developed countries. This proposal was formally circulated on 19 December, which proved to be an eventful day.

In addition to the circulation of the aforementioned proposal, the morning started with a visit to the fifth committee of Harri Holkeri, President of the General Assembly. He urged the members to press ahead in the few remaining days to agree on the scales of assessment. That very evening the Secretary-General also appeared at 7:30 p.m. He urged the delegates present to move with all deliberate speed in agreeing on the scales of assessment, pointing out the adverse consequences of not doing so. After the PGA and the Secretary-General had made their statements, several delegates intervened; some to agree on the need to move forward, others to take issue with the whole idea.

Also on 19 December, the G77 met in order to consider adopting a common position on the scales of assessment. The Arab Group proposed, through their president, the delegate of Egypt, that the scale of assessments on peacekeeping be postponed for the resumed session of March. The Río Group explained their proposal on peacekeeping (in a somewhat defensive manner, since Colombia was severely criticized by some delegations for hosting the closed weekend meetings), pointing out the potential trade-offs that existed in considering both scales simultaneously, thus expressing their rejection of the Arab Group's proposal. While a diversity of views was expressed, no common position emerged on any issue.

At the same time, the Río Group introduced on 19 December its formal proposal on the peacekeeping scale to the fifth committee. Among its features: eight levels (instead of the then-existing four) to differentiate between various categories of countries; a phasing-in period of three years for some countries, and a date of application of 1 July 2001 (Argentina had defended the idea of postponing the application of the new scale until 1 January 2002, and the mid-year entry date was a compromise).

The final decisive stage

The events described in the previous paragraphs set the stage for the rather dramatic developments that took place between 20 and 23 December. During this lapse of time, the fifth committee was in session on average some 20 hours a day, with a large array of ambassadors in attendance. On Wednesday 20 December, the proposal of 19 December was considered. It received much criticism, especially because some high-income countries had been included in the phase-in scheme (Singapore and Korea, among them), an idea that the developed countries rejected.

The G77, which, as indicated above, had been unable to agree on a common position the previous day, nevertheless came forward with an alternative proposal, which basically called for maintaining the existing methodology, including the 25 percent ceiling and the use of debt stock instead of debt flow for purposes of the debt burden calculations. Other countries that were adversely affected by the base period of 4.5 years expressed their preference to return to a six-year base period. A perfunctory interpretation of the debate would have led the listener to conclude that the tabled proposal was "dead in the water", given the large number and the intensity of the objections raised, but a more careful reading revealed that most of the criticism was intended as a last-minute effort to mitigate some aspects that had been found objectionable during the whole process, in the context of a growing realization that the essence of the US initiative would prevail.

There was some confusion as to what to do next, and a recess was called. The G77 went off to caucus, and the author suggested a meeting of the "friends of the chair" to discuss strategy. By then it was 11 p.m., most of the ambassadors were hanging around in the halls, and even the Secretary-General arrived after dinner to peruse the situation. The G77 demands had boiled down to two matters: insisting on the phasing-in mechanism for adversely affected developing countries, and the use of debt stock instead of debt flow for the debt burden calculations. The acceptance of the highly contested reduction of the ceiling for the regular budget appeared to be accepted, albeit with resignation.

Then, an extraordinary meeting took place in conference room E, in which the general outlines of the scale of assessments methodology were worked out, with the help of Egypt's fifth committee delegate, Ayman M. Elgammal. There were strong exchanges between ambassadors Holbrooke and Levitte (the latter aided by Jeremy Greenstock), around the matter of addressing the concerns of the G77, represented in this particular meeting by Teniola Olusegun Apata, alternate permanent representative of Nigeria. It was clear that few resources were available to finance the phasing-in scheme: the US offered the equivalent of the 3 percent that would be saved in the first year due to the reduction of the ceiling (later it was announced that Ted Turner, the main benefactor of the United Nations Foundation, had donated the amount of $ 34 million to the State Department for this purpose). The Russian Federation announced that it would make available around 0.4 percent a year for three years for the same purpose (the difference between its calculated scale of 0.804 and its voluntary commitment to pay 1.200). No additional funds were forthcoming, in spite of the entreaties of the G77 spokesperson. This led to some rather acrimonious confrontations, which went essentially unresolved. Still, by 2 a.m., the broad outlines of a proposal had been hammered out. The author offered to present a concrete scale the following day for all the delegations' consideration.

On Thursday 21 December, the new proposal was tabled. The discussions took on a distinctly North-South cleavage. The G77 insisted on the phase-in scheme for its members, on the debt stock issue, and on the possibility of freezing the methodology for nine years. Korea voluntarily reduced its phase-in to one year, and Singapore backed off altogether in asking for the phase-in. Since the supply of funds was short, demand had to be pared. But only part of the discussion was on substance; the other component formed part of the often criticized, but also misunderstood and often useful ritual intrinsic to multilateral diplomacy at the UN, in which lengthy discussions gradually yield to a consensus which rarely satisfies anyone, but does allow for moving on.

At the same time, the scale of assessments for peacekeeping operations was examined, basically following the Río Group proposal. The main issue of contention was the insistence of the G77, on behalf of Singapore and some of the Gulf States, that a new (ninth) level be introduced, with a 15 percent discount. The compromise reached was an acceptance of the creation of a ninth category, but with a 7.5 percent discount. Again, strong disagreements were followed by compromises, and by 2 a.m. a virtual agreement had been reached, on both scales, subject to a final revision later in the day. The European Union, as well as Canada, Australia, and New Zealand, had accepted contributing to the phasing-in scheme, not by adding new resources, but by phasing in their own contributions, perhaps by front-loading their allotted share in the first two years, but recuperating the excess payments in the last year.

Friday 22 December had been set as the deadline to conclude the General Assembly. Delegates were convened for 11 a.m. in order to begin considering the peacekeeping scale and its draft resolution, to be followed in the afternoon by the regular budget scale and its draft resolution. However, a new glitch appeared: the preparation of the paper work and documentation proved to be more difficult than originally thought. The phasing-in scheme, and its implications for contributors and users, was quite complex, and it took the better part of the day to prepare the tables. Thus, instead of 11 a.m., work did not get underway for the peacekeeping scale until 6 p.m. and for the regular budget scale until much later that night.

Further, while progress was being achieved, new difficulties arose. First, the G77 re-opened the question of freezing the methodology for nine years, and finally settled for six years. Second, the Republic of Korea belatedly announced that it had new instructions from its ministry of foreign relations to scale back its original offer for peacekeeping operations. And, finally, a dispute developed between the US, the EU, and China regarding the exact implications of combining a new scale of assessment for the regular budget that would go into effect on 1 January 2001, with a new scale of assessment for peacekeeping which would not go into effect until 1 July 2001. How would the assessments be calculated in this interim period?

It took all night to work out solutions to these intricate questions. The recesses were longer than the sessions, while consultations were taking place between delegates and their capitals, and among delegates (and possibly among capitals). Between 2 a.m. and dawn, many delegates suggested adjourning, and convening for another day, but others felt that the window of opportunity might close. Thus, a new recess was declared while, first, the Korean ambassador received new instructions (no doubt the product of bilateral prodding on the part of the United States), and, second, the P-5 worked out an interim arrangement among their countries on how peacekeeping would be financed between 1 January and 30 June 2001, until both new scales came into full effect. By dawn of Saturday 23 December, agreements had been reached, and at noon of the same day both resolutions and scales had been approved by the fifth committee, and, shortly thereafter, ratified by the General Assembly.

An assessment of the outcome

The prior narrative holds many lessons for the different elements at play in multilateral diplomacy at the United Nations, especially when the stakes are high. First of all, personalities do count. There is little doubt that the driving force behind the two scales was the relentless initiative of the United States, and especially the personal interventions of Richard Holbrooke. Although all public proclamations heard at the UN were opposed to the lowering of the ceiling of the regular budget scale, numerous colleagues understood that they were inexorably headed for just such a scenario. What was in doubt was, first, exactly how messy the process would be; and, second, to what extent the concerns of other governments would be accommodated.

One could not entirely discount that a unified opposition to lowering of the ceiling could derail the US initiative, with whatever ensuing consequences that would entail for the United Nations. However, most ambassadors understood that bringing the ceiling down was bad enough, in terms of the capacity to pay principle, but that not doing so might be even more damaging in the long run, measured in terms of the US-UN relation. Another important point to make borrows from George Orwell's celebrated phrase from *Animal Farm*, that "some animals are more equal than others." The leverage displayed by the United States in "getting its way" was not lost on anyone.

Still another implicit issue that came up was the consequences of letting the forces of inertia dictate policies when the intricacies of multilateral diplomacy made adaptation to change too difficult. For example, the peacekeeping scale depended on an *ad hoc* arrangement which had not been updated since 1973. The intellectual case for seeking agreement on a new scale was therefore compelling, but so too was the resistance it engendered. The US insisted that both scales must be agreed to, as contemplated in the Helms-Biden legislation; many developing countries preferred to concentrate on the regular budget scale, and repeatedly floated the idea of postponing consideration of peacekeeping until the resumed session of March, if not later. However, what avoided this later idea from taking shape was, first, the European Union's adamant insistence that both scales had to be considered together, given their internal linkages; and, second, the Río Group had also bought into the idea, thus weakening a united G77 opposition.

An additional and important element in the negotiations was that almost each of the major players came into the negotiations with "red lines." The US wanted the ceiling to be reduced to 22 percent. Japan put everyone on notice that their contribution to the regular budget could not go beyond a threshold of 20 percent. The European Union repeatedly reminded delegations that their contribution was way above their share of global GNP, and that they would not contribute one extra cent to the regular budget. And most developing countries understandably refused to pick up the slack left by the United States, pointing out the perverse situation of "subsidizing" what up to the present had been the US contribution. In other words, there seemed to be little room for compromise. But pragmatism appears to have prevailed for the greater good of the United Nations. The primary consideration was putting the US-UN relation on a firmer footing, but the recuperation of a significant proportion of the US arrears also played an important role in persuading most countries to give the US initiative serious consideration, especially in response to the numerous *démarches* made at capitals.

A few countries accepted their responsibility of carrying a greater burden both in the regular budget and in peacekeeping. But their proclamations usually were conditioned to avoid abrupt increases. The Republic of Korea and Singapore initially asked for a phased-in increase over a number of years (they subsequently backed off). China indicated it was willing to increase its contribution, but within "reasonable limits." India and Brazil took the same position. In general, the middle income countries, and China as well, resented being "targeted" for large increases. The EU was not quite as generous, and played with different combinations of decreasing the low per capita income adjustment—the "gradient"—so as to increase numerous countries' contribution. "Bottom lines" also appeared even within the group of countries that accepted—at the conceptual level—the need to increase their contributions to both scales. Brazil effectively lobbied for limits to its increase, arguing domestic fiscal difficulties. Argentina did the same for its contribution to peacekeeping. As already noted, Singapore and Korea put limits to what they could contribute. China took refuge in its principled foreign policy, stating that it wished to be treated like every other country, no better and no worse.

The trick, then, was to capitalize on the political acceptance that concessions had to be made to the US, within the severe limits described above. Most of the ground-work was undertaken by the US itself, through bilateral representations which reportedly included exerting a great deal of pressure, as well as the profuse use of the media to its own benefit. But the final outcome had to be resolved in the fifth committee, which has its own logic in building a consensus in a multilateral context. In a way, the situation was ideally suited for a United Nations-style negotiation, since many delegations had, at one level, accepted the inevitability of the outcome, but, at another level, strenuously and sincerely resisted it. The space that the fifth committee offered for these delegations to ventilate their frustrations, make their own (minor) demands, and, in general, feel part of the consensus building, became a significant intrinsic element to the historic agreements reached in the final days of negotiation.

It could be argued that one of the major strategic triumphs of the negotiation was to understand when the fifth committee needed to be circumvented (in the very initial stages) and when it needed to be taken fully into account (in the final stages). Two particular tactical challenges were: first, maintaining a dispassionate and business-like atmosphere in the committee (given the potentially incendiary nature of the topics at hand), and, second, arranging for a "soft landing" of the parallel consultations in the committee. Both challenges were successfully met.

As to the scale of the regular budget, solutions were found through gradual approximations. At one point, the EU faced its own dilemma, derived from its position of negotiating jointly by establishing its own maximum threshold of 15 percent. The shift in the base period calculation, from 6 years to 4.5 years, benefited France, Germany, and Italy, in that their contributions went down, but seriously affected the United Kingdom, whose contribution went up given that country's improving economic performance at the global stage in the preceding years. Surprisingly, it appears that there had never been a discussion on how the bill would be distributed within the EU membership.

At the end of the day, most countries and grouping remained quite close to their "bottom line." The US made two relatively minor concessions. First, it provided the "sweetener" of $35 million (thanks to Ted Turner's largesse) which, rather than benefit all member states on a *pro rata* basis, was destined to finance part of the phasing-out scheme. Second, it softened its demands for the peacekeeping scale (its contribution did not rigorously comply with Helms-Burton legislation, since it would be above 27 percent, rather than 25 percent). Japan was too close to its bottom line (19.5 percent) to contemplate any concessions. The EU made a very minor concession, as a group, and through some of its member countries, by allocating part of the reduction that some of the countries had experienced due to the shortening of the base period to financing the phase-in, during the first two years, but recuperating such an allocation in the last year. Canada, Australia, and New Zealand, with their usual generosity, did the same. And China played a constructive role by accepting a significant increase in its contribution to the regular budget, and not asking for any special consideration. The same can be said for the Russian Federation.

For their part, the developing countries (and a few developed countries) got something in return. First, some were allowed to phase-in their increase over a three-year period (Brazil, Chile, Colombia, Iran, Iraq, Nigeria, Thailand, Uruguay, Uzbekistan, Vietnam, the Czech Republic, Poland, and Korea; the latter, for one year). Second, the developed countries reluctantly accepted that debt stock should be used for the discount on debt burden. And, third, the methodology was frozen in place for six years, instead of for three (in fact, by 2015 the same methodology had prevailed for 15 years).

Was there really a massive transfer of the burden of maintaining the regular budget away from developed countries and to the detriment of developing countries? Table 3.1 reveals the percentages accruing to each country or group of countries for the 2000 budget and for 2001.

Within the Canz group, it was Canada that assumed a slight increase in its contribution. The same can be said for Norway. Thus, two developed countries partially mitigated the decrease in the contribution

Table 3.1 Ratio of contribution of indicated countries or group of countries to the regular budget of the Unite Nations (percent of total), 2000–2001

	2000	2001
United States	25.000	22.000
European Union	36.374	36.768
Japan	20.573	19.629
Canz Group	3.836	4.451
Norway	0.610	0.650
Total	86.393	83.498

of the US and Japan. The rest of the 2.895 percent decrease of developed countries' contributions to the budget was absorbed by Central European and developing countries. The Russian Federation, China, Brazil, Korea, and Singapore made up the bulk of this transfer (2.377 percent of the differential); the other 0.518 percent was assumed by the other 162 countries, although the lower-income countries did not experience any increase in their contributions.

Conclusion

In summary, everyone got a little: the US, Japan, the EU, and the G77. Even Cuba got a bit of satisfaction, by being allowed in the final session to deliver a blistering attack on the whole process, which was described as an imperial imposition on the membership. However, the Cuban ambassador, Bruno Rodriguez, was careful to point out that in spite of his rejection of the whole process his country had decided to join the consensus, in an act of solidarity with the rest of the G77.

It can further be stated that some of the mutual concessions made during the "horse-trading" of the last three days of the session did not seriously compromise the integrity, transparency, and fairness of the scale of assessments methodology. In fact, if taken together with the introduction of an updated scale of assessments for peacekeeping, the way that the United Nations is financed experienced a major reform in 2000.

Finally, the most difficult question posed at the time was whether the battle was worth it. On that occasion, the verdict was not at all clear. Subsequent events suggest that the reply would be in the affirmative. The arrears of the United States were paid in full within four years, the dust settled relatively quickly, and member states learned to live with their new budgetary commitments to the United Nations. However, the lingering memory of the epic battles described in this narrative have contributed to the reluctance to continue updating the way the contributions to the UN budget are apportioned, which explains why the decision adopted on the morning of 23 December 2000 still defines the scales of assessment both for the regular budget and for peacekeeping operations until the present.

Notes

1 The author has written on this topic previously, although in a different context and with a different content. See: Gert Rosenthal, "The Scale of Assessments of the United Nations' Budget: A Case Study of How the United States Exercises Its Leverage in a Multilateral Setting," *Global Governance* 10, No. 3 (2004): 353–372.

2 These provisions are in Division C, Section 2101 entitled "United Nations Reform", in the FY1999 State Department Authorization of the Budget.

3 For the uninitiated in UN matters, the United Nations actually has two separate budgets. The "regular budget," with its own scale of assessments based on the principle of capacity to pay covers all recurrent cost of the Secretariat, world-wide, including the rapidly growing portfolio of "Special Political Missions." The peacekeeping budget is more flexible, since it reflects the rapidly changing circumstances that require the presence of peace operations, and where the scale of assessments contemplates larger relative contributions on the part of permanent members of the Security Council.

4 These efforts went so far as to parade Senators Jesse Helms and then Senator Joe Biden through the UN Headquarters on 20 January 2000. They participated in a meeting of the Security Council (a highly unusual occurrence) and at a luncheon offered by Secretary-General Kofi Annan. The announced purpose of the visit was to "improve US–UN relations." See: www.jesse helmscenter.org/archives-and-museum/online-exhibits/united-nations-reform -the-helms-biden-act/

5 Some of the major players in the negotiation were the following: Jean-David Levitte of France, who acted as the spokesperson for the European Union; Jeremy Greenstock of the UK, who started out staking a discreet distance from the EU position—more amenable to the US—and ended up as a "hard-liner" when he discovered belatedly that the UK would be assessed relatively more under the new scales than other EU partners; Yukio Satoh of Japan, who insisted that Japanese public opinion would not tolerate any level of contribution beyond 20 percent of the regular budget (unless, of course, Japan were awarded a permanent seat at the Security Council, in which case further flexibility could be offered); Sun joun-yung of the Republic of Korea, representing one of the countries "targeted" by the US to increase its contributions to both the regular budget and the peacekeeping budget; Wang Yingfan of China, who rejected the idea of being "targeted" as a major contributor, and insisted that China be treated equally with other developing countries; Sergey V. Lavrov of the Russian Federation, who was personally less involved than the other major players; Arthur C.I. Mbanefo, as well as Teniola Olusegun Apata of Nigeria, who

represented the G77 at the time; Penny Wensley of Australia; Gelson Fonseca Jr. of Brazil; Arnoldo Listre of Argentina; Alfonso Valdivieso of Colombia, who exercised the Presidency of the Río Group, and made common cause with Argentina and Brazil; Dumisani Shadrack Kumalo of South Africa, who acted as President of the Non-Aligned Movement; Kishore Mahbubani of Singapore; Kamalesh Sharma of India; Mohammad J. Samhan of United Arab Emirates; Ahmed Aboul Gheit of Egypt; Movses Abelian of Armenia, as facilitator of the informal consultations on the scale of assessments for peacekeeping; Frank Smyth, of Ireland, the facilitator of the informal consultations on the scale of assessments for the regular budget; Marc Gilpin, Secretary of the Committee on Contributions, and Joseph Acakpo-Satchivi, Secretary of the Fifth Committee.

6 That is also why many delegates view the fifth committee with dread, while the members of the committee feel quite empowered, given their unique expertise, which most of the Heads of Mission neither want to get involved with nor often even try to understand.

7 The *Río Group* was established in 1990 as an offshoot of the *Contadora Group* created in 1983 by Colombia, Mexico, Panama, and Venezuela to foster peace in Central America, and the so-called "support group" created in 1985 by Argentina, Brazil, Peru, and Uruguay. By the year 2000, the Río Group had expanded its membership to virtually all non-English speaking countries of the region (plus one representative of CARICOM), and its original purpose had been transformed into a Permanent Mechanism of Political Consultation. In 2010, the Group, which by then had the membership of all countries of the region, was transformed into the Community of Latin American and Caribbean States (CELAC). The first time the Río Group took on a role as a regional actor at the United Nations was for the scale of assessment discussions of 2000.

8 The methodology for the scale of assessments of the regular budget is based on capacity to pay. The indicator used is gross national product, an average for the "base period", which can be of three or six years, or of any other variant. GNP figures, in domestic currencies, are converted to dollars, usually based on market exchange rates. Countries below the threshold (usually average world GNP) are given an adjustment, called a "gradient," which in 2000 was of 80 percent. A further adjustment is made for debt burden. There is a minimum assessment rate of 0.001 percent and a maximum assessment rate for the LDC's of 0.01 percent. Finally, there is the ceiling of 25 percent that was the object of all the controversy. Thus, many variables can be manipulated to influence the scale.

9 The refraining of a detailed description of the complexities behind the scales of assessment is deliberate, since it sheds little light on the main points the author wishes to make. This information is, however, readily available. See, for example: United Nations, *Report of the Committee on Contributions, Seventy-second session, 4–29 June, 2012* (A/67/11, July 12, 2012); and, for the apportionment of the expenses of the peacekeeping operations budget: United Nations, *Implementation of General Assembly resolutions 55/235 and 55/236*, 23 December 2000, and the *Report of the Secretary-General* (A/67/224, 3 August 2012).

4 ECOSOC in 2003

A principal organ in search of its identity

- **The underlying dilemma**
- **Work program and its organization**
- **Highlights of the 2003 session**
- **Epilogue**
- **Conclusion**

Guatemala was elected to the Economic and Social Council on 26 October 2001, and joined it for a three-year period on 1 January 2002. The author was elected to be the senior vice-president,[1] under the expectation that he would assume the presidency in 2003, which in fact occurred. The rest of the members of the bureau in 2003 were Marjatta Rasi (Finland, and who became president in 2004), Murari Raj Sharma (Nepal), Abdul Mejid Hussein (Ethiopia), and Valery P. Kuchinsky (Ukraine). A very collegial atmosphere was developed in working together, and in distributing the work-load. Secretarial support was provided by a small but efficient staff, headed by Sarbuland Khan, with the assistance of Aliye Celik and Nikhil Seth.

It is not the purpose of this chapter to offer a detailed narrative of the events that occurred or the formal outputs of ECOSOC in 2003, since that information is available in the official documents.[2] Rather, in contrast to previous chapters which explore the dynamics of multilateral diplomacy at work through the shaping of specific events or decisions, here there is a more general exploration of systemic issues that affect the United Nations in the area of decision-making, especially of the so-called development pillar. This warrants a brief incursion into the relations between the three principal intergovernmental organs, as perceived from the vantage point of ECOSOC, and, more specifically as viewed from the author's privileged observatory as its president in 2003. His single overriding recollection is a permanent exercise in ascertaining and enhancing the relevance of the Council, often by complementing its mandated functions with more-or-less contrived activities designed to make a mark on the United Nations' agenda.

The underlying dilemma

That is not to suggest that some of those "contrived" activities were not useful or interesting, because many of them were, as is made clear below. But it was equally clear that almost since its founding, ECOSOC had suffered a type of identity crisis; a circumstance that has not been palpable either in the General Assembly, nor much less in the Security Council. The broad feeling of dissatisfaction with ECOSOC over the years, both among academics—one spoke about "the persistent unimportance of ECOSOC"—[3] and among member states, was manifested with periodic calls for either its "strengthening," its "reform," or even occasionally its extinction.[4] The recurring efforts to increase the relevance of the Council have run the gamut from changes in its rules of procedure, working methods, agenda, redefining its role, and enlarging its membership.

Over the years, different groups of experts and blue ribbon panels—some sponsored by the United Nations, others working independently—have addressed the matter.[5] In fact, some of the recommendations formulated over time by different proponents have been partially or fully implemented, especially during the past decade (2005–2015), but it is equally telling that many of those recommendations have not been put into practice, or that their systemic nature has not been fully acknowledged.[6] In other words, some of the difficulties identified are not necessarily restricted to ECOSOC, but affect the whole United Nations system that ECOSOC belongs to.

In large measure, the difficulties faced by this organ have been a consequence of its ambiguous relationship with the General Assembly, and especially the latter's second and third committees. Part of the ambiguity stemmed from the fact that, under Article 60 of the Charter, ECOSOC discharges its functions "under the authority of the General Assembly," while under Article 7(1) it does so as a principal organ of the United Nations, not subject to the authority of any other organ. In addition, there are several allusions to the links between ECOSOC and the General Assembly, including Articles 60, 62, 63, 64, and 66 whereby, in some cases ECOSOC virtually receives instructions from the General Assembly while, in others ECOSOC appears to be taking the initiative of formulating recommendations to the General Assembly. These apparent inconsistencies contained in the wording of the

Charter can be attributed to the fact that the original language in the draft of the Charter that emanated from the Dumbarton Oaks Proposals of 1944 contemplated the creation of ECOSOC as a subsidiary body of the General Assembly. It was during the San Francisco Conference that the idea of ECOSOC as a principal organ was born, but part of the drafting on the original intention seems to have survived together with the revisions incorporated in San Francisco.[7]

An additional feature that adds to the aforementioned "identity crisis" is born out of the permanent tension alluded to in previous chapters between universal bodies, such as those associated with the General Assembly, and more restricted bodies, such as ECOSOC and especially the Security Council. As already mentioned, some countries invoke transparency to promote the idea that all the work of the intergovernmental organs should be carried out in "committees of the whole;" i.e., with all member states of the UN represented. ECOSOC, with its 54 elected members (by the General Assembly), has by definition not met that requirement, although in recent years concessions have been made by placing under the Council—in association with the General Assembly—new subsidiary bodies, such as the High-Level Political Forum and the forum on financing for development follow-up, both mentioned below. These bodies are open to all members of the United Nations, even when they meet under the aegis of the Council.

Functions and interactions with other organs

The "functions and powers" of ECOSOC, as enumerated in Articles 62 to 66 of the Charter, characterize this organ as a forum for reflection on development issues,[8] for offering policy guidance (through its recommendations), and for undertaking both a normative role (draft conventions) and an advocacy role. In other words, the Council can have an impact by fostering the debate and influencing policy makers. However, as is also the case for the General Assembly, its decisions are not binding on member States. Again, some of these functions clearly overlap with the remit of the General Assembly.

While the systemic overlapping of functions occurs in virtually all sectors, on occasion a division of responsibilities between the two organs can be worked out. In 2003, ECOSOC assumed primary (but not exclusive) responsibility in a few areas, mostly derived from its subsidiary bodies. The first area was related to the traditional agenda of the Council, in fostering debates (mostly during the high-level segment), and in the follow-up of major conferences.

A second area in which ECOSOC assumed prime responsibility was in nominally overseeing the activities of the five regional commissions. "Nominally," because the oversight was limited to receiving a yearly report from each of the commissions, which was the basis for a brief—at most half a day—discussion on the performance of the regional commissions between the members of the Council.

The third remit was related to the activities carried out by the functional commissions (statistics, population, human rights, social development, status of women, narcotic drugs, crime prevention, and others).[9] This was perhaps the single most significant area of specialization of the Council, but it must be acknowledged that, at least in 2003, the level and depth of oversight offered was similar to that described in the previous paragraph related to the regional commissions. Indeed, most of the subsidiary bodies had shown, at least up to 2003, a tendency to work with a high level of independence.

An additional function assigned to ECOSOC appears in Articles 63 and 64 of the Charter, the former indicating that the Council "may coordinate the activities of the specialized agencies through consultation with and recommendations to such agencies ..." However, the Council had been singularly unsuccessful in contributing to meaningful system-wide coherence; rather, the same pattern of pro-forma reports from each agency and a brief general discussion were the usual modalities of compliance with this remit, added to a debate on a specific topic during the operational activities for development segment (see below).

An additional and significant function was derived from Article 71 of the Charter, which in effect designates ECOSOC as the gateway to the United Nations for non-governmental organizations. The modality is vested in the Committee on Non Governmental Organizations, made up of 19 members, who collectively are responsible for granting consultative status to non-governmental organizations (NGOs). At the time, about half the members of this Committee favored restricting consultative status to new applicants, while the other half encouraged it, generating some internal tension in this specialized body; tensions which spilled over to the wider membership of ECOSOC and the United Nations at large.

The work of the Human Rights Commission deserves special mention, since the Charter specifically assigns to ECOSOC the function of promoting respect for, and observance of, human rights (Articles 62 and 68), although in cooperation with the General Assembly and even the by then inactive Trusteeship Council. Indeed, the Human Rights Commission—a subsidiary body of ECOSOC—was at the time the main forum for debating this highly sensitive topic (and the precursor of the Human Rights Council established in 2005). This in itself generated some divisiveness within ECOSOC, since a controversial political cleavage appeared—mostly between countries with democratic orientations and those with a more authoritarian inclination—that clashed with the over-all thrust of ECOSOC, which pursued international economic cooperation, an aspect of the UN agenda that seems to generate less intense controversy.

The matter of the links between the Council and the General Assembly has already been discussed above. At best, the Charter is subject to different interpretations on the matter of the division of responsibilities between both organs, and how these interact, but Article 60 does establish at least an implicit hierarchy which seems to place the General Assembly above the Council.

As to the links between ECOSOC and the Security Council, Article 65 limits the former's role to furnishing information to the latter or assisting the Security Council "upon its request." Until quite recently, the Security Council's request for assistance was a rare occurrence.[10] Indeed, in practice the relationship between these two organs has not been devoid of tension, as the Security Council expanded its thematic agenda, linking development and environmental issues with their potential for threatening international peace and security. This tendency was perceived by many as an encroachment of the Security Council on the purviews of both ECOSOC and the General Assembly. An example at that time (2003) was the convening by the Security Council in July 2000 to examine the spread of HIV/AIDS in Africa, arguably a subject closer to ECOSOC's traditional agenda. Tellingly, the agenda item was called: "On the Responsibility of the Security Council in the Maintenance of International Peace and Security: HIV/AIDS and International Peacekeeping Operations."

Work program and its organization

The calendar of meetings of ECOSOC traditionally followed a fairly rigid format. At the beginning of the year there was a formal meeting for the "changing of the guard," where the outgoing and incoming presidents delivered their respective messages. Shortly thereafter, a brief organizational meeting was held, usually first at an informal level, followed by a formal session to approve the years' work program. In March, working groups met to brainstorm and prepare the outcome of the regular session; in 2003 the session was to be held in Geneva from 30 June to 25 July.[11] Another important event was the yearly spring meeting held since 1998 between ECOSOC, the Bretton Woods Institutions, the World Trade Organization, and, since 2004, UNCTAD.

In the lead-up to the regular session of 2003, a few informal meetings were held in April and May, mostly to agree on the draft ministerial declaration to be produced in Geneva. Finally, there were some resumed sessions in the last quarter of the year, since at that time ECOSOC organized its work in accordance with the calendar year (as does the Security Council), while the General Assembly had a cycle that, as is well known, begins in September of each year. In summary, the bulk of ECOSOC's work was concentrated in a single four-week session.

That session also followed a fairly rigid format, which had been put in place since 1996.[12] It was organized in "segments" which started with a high-level segment, followed by a coordination segment of operational activities for development, a humanitarian affairs segment, and a "general segment."[13] It was customary for the president to preside the high-level segment, and each of the four vice-presidents to preside one of the remaining segments. Of course, additional meetings could be called to deal with other issues, such as the follow-up to United Nations conferences or on more specific issues, as occurred on several occasions during 2003.

ECOSOC's dedicated secretariat was spread thin during part of the year providing support to the different forums, both in preparing the documentation to facilitate decision-making on the part of the intergovernmental bodies as well as in keeping records. In that respect, the interaction between the secretariat and the member states was similar to that observed system-wide. This interaction was more intense at the level of the bureau, which among other aspects was responsible for implementing the decisions taken by the broader membership in its organizational session.

Highlights of the 2003 session

When the author assumed the presidency of the Council in 2003 he perceived the opportunity not only as a commitment to enhance the relevance of the work program for 2003, but also as an occasion to better understand the roots of the "identity crisis" of this principal forum, whose general contours are described in preceding paragraphs. Therefore, while his mindset was partially focused on discovering "what is wrong with ECOSOC?" he also understood that a more positive attitude was indispensable to rally constructive engagement among member states. Indeed, with the benefit of hindsight, some positive outcomes were achieved, a number of which are worth mentioning to illustrate the point, as well as to address the previous comment related to "contrived activities."

The first and probably most memorable event was the spring meeting with the Bretton Woods Institutions and other multilateral institutions. As mentioned previously, this practice had started in 1998, but the April 14 2003 gathering was of special significance, since it was held almost exactly one year after the celebration of the International Conference on Financing for Development (see Chapter 2). The event therefore offered a first opportunity to hold a dialogue between the United Nations (represented by ECOSOC), the World Bank, the International Monetary Fund, and the World Trade Organization, all represented by the highest level of management as well as members of their respective intergovernmental executive boards. Both the Monterrey Consensus and numerous previous ECOSOC resolutions placed issues of coherence, coordination, and cooperation related to the follow-up as the center-pieces of the discussion. The dialogue was geared to identify progress, or the lack thereof, in complying with the commitments contained in the Monterrey Consensus, in each of its six chapters.[14]

The 2003 dialogue was able to convene numerous delegations at the highest level. For example, special mention should be made of the Minister of Finance of South Africa and chairperson of the Bretton Wood's Development Committee, Trevor Manuel, and of the minister for economic cooperation and development of Germany, Heidemarie Wieczorek Zeul, since both exercised strong leadership in the plenary sessions as well as in the four round tables organized for interactive discussions. It was one of the occasions in the author's recollection when a meaningful and even uplifting dialogue took place between delegations representing both the economic and the foreign relations portfolios of their respective governments on the broader topic of financing for development and the more specific matter of relations between the United Nations and the Bretton Woods Institutions.[15]

A second aspect which produced some tangible results on the ground in 2003 was derived from the ad hoc advisory group on African countries emerging from conflict, especially referring to Burundi and Guinea Bissau. This mechanism, created the previous year,[16] and a precursor of what was to become the Peacebuilding architecture established in 2005, gave rise to two activities, on Burundi and Guinea-Bissau, which offered both countries a source of advocacy, including the promotion of meetings of officials of both countries with the donor community.[17] During 2003, and as a direct result of this mechanism, UNDP helped organize a donor conference in Brussels for Burundi which proved to be quite successful.[18]

A third aspect that had a visible impact was derived from the Permanent Forum for Indigenous Issues, an advisory body to the Economic and

Social Council established in 2000,[19] but whose first meeting was only held in 2002. This forum, constituted by 16 members elected in their personal capacity, has a mandate to discuss indigenous issues related to economic and social development, culture, the environment, education, health, and human rights. By 2003, only its second session, it had accumulated an impressive convening capacity, attracting hundreds of observers from indigenous communities and from non-governmental organizations. It was the first important forum for indigenous issues to hold meetings in New York, since previous bodies gravitated around indigenous rights, and functioned in Geneva under the aegis of the Human Rights Commission.

Finally, it must be acknowledged that ECOSOC had made a contribution to what perhaps the United Nations does best in its development pillar: to explore emerging development issues and make them understandable not only for policy-makers, but also for the proverbial man on the street. In other words, the debate ultimately does impact on public awareness, and also on policy prescriptions. But the United Nations has multiple arenas where the policy debate can and is undertaken, and here the issue of overlapping and duplication appears front-and-center. It could be argued that the global forum best suited for a serious policy debate is the Economic and Social Council, given its mandate, its composition, and its work ethic. But it could also be argued that while the Council has sometimes risen to the occasion, and made a significant impact on the real world, this has not always been the case.

In this respect, the author believed at the time that the so-called "High-level segment" of 2003 was successful and that a serious debate had ensued, producing a substantive ministerial declaration (the topic was "promoting an integrated approach to rural development in developing countries for poverty eradication and sustainable development").[20] At the same time, it became clear that in sorting out "who does what" within the United Nations in the economic and social fields, ECOSOC was both a victim and a contributor of the fragmentation that has characterized the organization, in spite of the subsequent vision of "delivering as one."[21] The lack of coordination and coherence that have bedeviled the United Nations in the past (with some ups and downs along the way) and which continue to affect it to this day, explain to a large degree why its work is compartmentalized or fragmented. This has indeed been a major flaw of multilateral diplomacy. Numerous resolutions meant to address this issue, adopted by the General Assembly in subsequent years, have on the whole not helped to clarify the aforementioned ambiguities.[22]

Moreover, two additional aspects that are systemic to all inter-governmental bodies of the United Nations have contributed to compromising the relevance of ECOSOC. The first is the continuous expansion of the agenda, as new emerging issues are addressed, without necessarily abandoning pre-existing issues. During 2003, for example, ECOSOC adopted 64 resolutions and 115 decisions on a wide variety of topics, many of which originated in the Council's subsidiary bodies. The vast majority of these 179 formal outputs, in addition to the ministerial declaration, emanated from the four week substantive session.

The second aspect is related to the ritualistic working methods, where prepared statements prevail over engagement and interactive dialogue. The assigned working days did not appear to be enough to accommodate serious consideration and discussion of the large and diverse range of topics that usually crowd the agenda, especially of the general segment, which was basically concerned with the management aspects of the subsidiary bodies. As an example, in carrying out its role of coordination, either system-wide or only with its own subsidiary bodies, the Council organized meetings where typically the reporting body presented a formal statement, followed by interventions of member states. These interventions often gravitated around polite comments and sometimes contained polite questions. The excessive ritual, or insufficient substance, in much of the carrying out of ECOSOC's broad mandates, was the result of ingrained habits, an excessive number of topics to be addressed in a limited period of time, and, sometimes, a perverse interaction between delegates and the secretariat, whereby the secretariat seeks friendly constituencies to support its reports. In short, it appeared that formality or ritual often trumped serious oversight on the part of member states.

In balance, the author felt that the regular 2003 session was successful by the traditional (fairly modest) standards that ECOSOC had established for itself, given the systemic difficulties that have afflicted it almost since its creation and the additional institutional shortcomings it faced. This was particularly so for the high-level segment: its format, content, level of representation, and especially the output of the policy dialogue were reasonably satisfactory. The humanitarian and operational segments were also on a par with the sessions of preceding years. And even the coordination segment served its main purpose regarding follow-up to the outcomes of the major United Nations conferences and summits.

The most glaring shortcomings appeared in the general segment. It was under this segment, for example, that reports were received from the regional commissions, the functional commissions, the standing committees, and the expert bodies, as well as the programs and agencies. Numerous pro-forma reports were received and commented on in a perfunctory and sometimes disjointed debate. In 2003, when the session was held in Geneva, numerous New-York based delegates returned to their duty station after a week, leaving more junior delegates to deal with the final segments. During the last week, the president had to repeatedly beseech briefers and delegates to limit their remarks to a few minutes, entirely missing the point that this was the only opportunity during the year for ECOSOC to exercise its oversight functions and to promote greater coherence in what the different bodies were doing. It came as no surprise, then, to witness first-hand the inability of the Council to coordinate even its own subsidiary bodies, and much less so the activities of the programs and specialized agencies.

In sum, it was clear that a more critical assessment was in order, mainly to identify what steps could be taken in the future to address the systemic issues already alluded to. Accordingly, the author, in his capacity as president of the Council, prepared a memorandum which was shared with all members of ECOSOC on 10 September 2003.[23] The memorandum is rather extended, but its essence can be summarized in one central paradox. On the one hand, the meeting was too long to keep the undivided attention and motivation of delegates during the full four weeks of its duration. On the other hand, it was too short to do justice to each and every item on the extensive agenda. This paradox was due to the fact that the Council historically concentrated the bulk of its substantive activities in one relatively long but uninterrupted session. As already stated, this became particularly evident during the general segment, where much of the oversight mandate of the Council is to be carried out.

The memorandum ended in a set of recommendations to further enhance and strengthen the work of the Council. In the area of working methods, it proposed re-grouping or streamlining the agenda between the different segments, to better reflect the different functions of the Council. The main thrust of this re-grouping would be to limit the items of what was called the "general segment" to the oversight or management functions of the Council over its subsidiary bodies. It also proposed extending the Council's substantive activities over a longer time-span, recommending a more rational distribution of holding different segments during the year so as to maximize the Council's capacity to prepare for its work and deliver timely responses and outputs. The memorandum also addressed the irrationality of continuing the practice of alternating the venue of the sessions between New York and Geneva.

A separate recommendation was to suggest transferring the Human Rights Commission to the purview of the General Assembly. The reason was that human rights were a cross-cutting issue and one of the core pillars of the United Nations' activities. The matter merited more in its institutional expression than being relegated to a subsidiary body of ECOSOC. Further, most debates in the Council were shaped by the desire of promoting international cooperation in the economic, social, and environmental sectors, and those debates were generally marked by a positive atmosphere, while, as already stated, the debates in the Human Rights Commission often took on a highly controversial and even confrontational tone, which sometimes poisoned the atmosphere in which other agenda items were being considered.

The memorandum was not intended to spur immediate reaction, but rather was offered to initiate a debate on overcoming the "identity crisis" alluded to earlier. However, the author was pleased to note that in subsequent years, many of those recommendations were put into effect, notably in September 2013, when the General Assembly adopted the already cited resolution 68/1. That is not to claim that the aforementioned memorandum was the detonator of decisions taken exactly ten years after it was circulated, but presumably it did influence in some small way the important events that occurred in the intervening years since the memorandum first saw light.

Epilogue

Indeed, a small epilogue is warranted to this chapter, since its narrative is limited to events that transpired in 2003. In fact, several important decisions were taken in subsequent years, and especially in 2005 with the adoption of the Summit Outcome Document, which somewhat altered the role of ECOSOC and holds the potential for enhancing its relevance.

Among the initiatives put in place in the Outcome Document that impacted directly on the work of ECOSOC several aspects can be mentioned. In addition to its calling for an enhanced role for the Council in general,[24] it also created a new Development Cooperation Forum, made up of the 54 member states of EOSOC, to meet on a biennial basis to review trends in international development cooperation.

In addition, two new bodies were created, and these would ultimately absorb some activities carried out by ECOSOC up to then. The first, as already stated, was the conversion of the Human Rights Commission, a subsidiary body of the Economic and Social Council, into the Human Rights Council, as a subsidiary body of the General

Assembly.[25] The second was the creation of a Peacebuilding Commission, designed to carry out and expand on activities entrusted up to that point to the Economic and Social Council in the areas of advocacy for African countries emerging from conflict, as well as advocacy for Haiti.[26] The creation of the Peacebuilding Commission, its Support Office and the Peacebuilding Fund were not designed to replace any of ECOSOC's work, but rather complement it. The Commission was conceived as an advisory body made up of 31 members, of which seven each are proposed by the three principal intergovernmental organs, including ECOSOC.

Another subsequent development of note was the creation, in 2010, of the United Nations Entity for Gender Equality and the Empowerment of Women (UN-Women),[27] which, again, was not designed to replace, but rather complement the Commission on the Status of Women, a subsidiary body of ECOSOC with a long and distinguished history in mobilization and advocacy for the advancement of women.

But perhaps the three most important developments with a potential to strengthen ECOSOC occurred quite recently. The first, already alluded to, was a far-reaching reform proposal relating to the organization of ECOSOC's annual work program and working methods, adopted by the General Assembly through resolution 68/1 on 20 September 2013. Instead of following the customary uninterrupted four week format, the Council's work is to be distributed between various gatherings and offering a prospect of a more coherent approach to meet its various functions in the areas of coordination, policy review, policy dialogue, and coordination, as well as the follow-up activities of the international development goals agreed at the major United Nations conferences and summits. It should be pointed out that the resolution made clear that: "the arrangements set forth ... should not lead to an increase in the number of meeting days currently provided for the Economic and Social Council" (point 4 of annex).[28]

Further, a positive step was taken in ending the practice of holding sessions every other year in Geneva—an expensive and rather inefficient proposition—by deciding that only the humanitarian affairs segment would continue to be held in alternate venues between New York and Geneva (a defensible decision, given that many of the humanitarian agencies are based in that city). The Council is tasked to create synergy and coherence as well as avoiding duplication between its deliberations and those of the high-level political forum on sustainable development. It is further tasked to conduct an annual dialogue with the Executive Secretaries of the regional commissions.

Second, and most importantly, ECOSOC assumed an enhanced role, albeit shared with the General Assembly, since the creation of the high-level political forum to integrate the three dimensions of sustainable development.[29] The format and organizational aspects of this new universal forum, charged with providing political leadership, guidance, and recommendations for sustainable development, were subsequently adopted by the General Assembly on 9 July 2013, through resolution 67/290. The forum is to meet every four years under the auspices of the General Assembly at the level of heads of state and government, and in the intervening period on a yearly basis "under the auspices of the Economic and Social Council ... for a period of eight days, including a three-day ministerial segment to be held in the framework of the substantive session of the Council, building on and subsequently replacing the annual ministerial review as from 2016."[30]

Third, as noted earlier, ECOSOC was charged, together with the General Assembly, in follow-up activities of the Financing for Development process under the Monterrey Declaration. During the Third International Conference on Financing for Development, the Addis Ababa Action Agenda was adopted, and subsequently ratified by the General Assembly. The follow-up activities "will include an annual Economic and Social Council forum on financing for development follow-up with universal, intergovernmental participation, to be launched during the Council's current cycle. The forum's modalities of participation will be those utilized at the international conferences on financing for development."[31]

Not only do these three decisions adopted between 2013 and 2016 potentially provide a focused function for ECOSOC, but it is to be noted that the latter two forums have universal membership, even when they meet under the auspices of ECOSOC. Although it could be argued that the dual responsibility between the two principal organs irredeemably debilitates ECOSOC, it could equally be sustained that the partnership arrangement is positive in balance, since it addresses the fundamental tension of the past of "who does what" between the General Assembly and the Council.

Conclusion

In conclusion, the Economic and Social Council has faced during its lifetime a dilemma in defining its relation with the General Assembly.[32] New developments undertaken since 2005, and particularly since 2013, open at least a possibility to address these challenges. Certainly the new responsibilities entrusted to the high-level political forum will give

ECOSOC the opportunity to clarify its own institutional identity. On the other hand, the gradual and partial evolution of ECOSOC in the direction of intergovernmental bodies of 193 members (instead of 54) and the fact that the ownership of the forum—and also the Development Cooperation Forum—is shared with the General Assembly, may still result in a further weakening of the Council. Only time will tell whether the "identity crisis" will persist or even get worse, or rather whether it will be overcome. At the time of writing, the jury was still out on the matter.

Notes

1 The Presidency of ECOSOC rotates by regional groupings. The President in 2002 was Ivan Šimonović (Croatia), and it would be GRULAC's turn in 2003.

2 See: *Report of the Economic and Social Council for 2003*, General Assembly Official Records Fifty-eighth Session Supplement No. 3 (A/58/3/Rev.1), 7 October 2005.

3 Philip Kunig, "The Economic and Social Council" in *The Charter of the United Nations: A commentary,* Bruno Simma et al. (eds) Second Edition, Volume II, (Oxford: Oxford University Press, 2002), 1010, paragraph 53. The chapter on ECOSOC in the Third Edition of Simma's monumental work, written by Volker Röben, is not quite as blunt, but essentially makes the same points. See: *The Charter of the United Nations: A commentary,* Bruno Simma et al. (eds), Third Edition, (Oxford: Oxford University Press, 2012), 1670–1672, paragraphs 2 and 5.

4 "Fifty years is long enough to know what works and what does not work within any system. ECOSOC has not worked." Commission on Global Governance, *Our Global Neighborhood* (London: Oxford University Press, 1995), 278.

5 The author explored this topic previously in two separate publications. See: Gert Rosenthal, "The Economic and Social Council of the United Nations", Friedrich Ebert Stiftung, *Occasional Papers Series,* 15 (February 2005), especially part 5, "The Permanent Quest for Reform," 16–24; and, "Economic and Social Council" in *The Oxford Handbook on the United Nations,* Thomas G. Weiss and Sam Daws (eds), (Oxford: Oxford University Press: 2007), 136–148.

6 Another recent analysis of ECOSOC and proposals to strengthen same is contained in the Secretary-General's *Report on the Implementation of General Assembly resolution 61/16 on the Strengthening of the Economic and Social Council,* (A/67/736-E/2013/7), 4 February 2013.

7 Stephen C. Schlesinger, *Act of Creation* (Boulder, Col.: Westview Press, 2003), 259–260.

8 Although the word "development" does not appear in any of the Articles of Chapter X, it is used explicitly in Article 55(a) in the formulation "improving the standard of living, achieving full employment, and creating the conditions of economic and social progress and development."

9 Article 68 of the Charter.

10 Sydney D. Bailey and Sam Daws, *The Procedures of the UN Security Council*, Third Edition (Oxford: Clarendon Press, 1998), 301–303.

11 The previous practice of always holding ECOSOC sessions in Geneva was modified in the 1990s by a decision to alternate the sessions between New York (in even years) and Geneva (in odd years). This was a typical compromise solution to satisfy each of the constituencies that preferred the competing venues. Only in 2013 was the decision taken to hold most of the regular sessions (the humanitarian segment being the exception) in New York, as per General Assembly resolution 68/1, 18 September, 2013.

12 See: General Assembly resolutions 50/227, 24 May 1996 and 57/153, 16 December 2002.

13 This format was changed in 2013 under the same resolution 68/1 mentioned in endnote 11.

14 *Monterrey Consensus*, as adopted on 22 March 2002 and endorsed by the General Assembly in resolution 56/210B on 1 August 2002; see especially paragraph 69, section b.

15 For a more detailed report on the meeting, see: *Report of the Economic and Social Council for 2003*, 11–12.

16 Resolution 2002/1, 15 July 2002.

17 ECOSOC resolutions 2003/1, 31 January 2003 and 2003/16, 21 July 2003.

18 A similar advocacy role was played in the case of Haiti, through the creation of an ad hoc advisory group on that country through ECOSOC resolution 1999/4 of 7 May 1999. The advisory group is still active at the time of writing.

19 Resolution 2000/22, 28 July 2000.

20 *Report of the Economic and Social Council for 2003*, 19–26.

21 Report of the High-level Panel on United Nations System-wide Coherence in the areas of development, humanitarian assistance and the environment, *Delivering as one*, (A/61/583, 20 November 2006).

22 See, for example: General Assembly resolutions 45/177, 19 December 1990; 45/264, 13 May 1991; 46/235, 13 April 1992; 48/162, 20 December 1993; 50/227, 24 May 1996 and 57/270B, 23 June 2003.

23 Memorandum circulated by the President of the Economic and Social Council to all members of the Council, *Proposal to Strengthen the Role of ECOSOC*, September 10 2003. The contents of the Memorandum can be revisited on: www.un.org/en/ecosoc/meetings/docs/presentation.rosenthal. pdf, 7 May 2004.

24 General Assembly resolution 60/1, 16 September 2005, paragraph 155. "We ... recognize the need for a more effective Economic and Social Council as a principal body for coordination, policy review, policy dialogue and recommendations on issues of economic and social development, as well as for implementation of the international development goals agreed at the major United Nations conferences and summits, including the Millennium Development Goals ..."

25 The Council was created by the General Assembly through resolution 60/251, 15 March 2006.

26 The Commission was created by the General Assembly and the Security Council through joint resolutions A/60/180-S/1645(2005), 20 December 2005.

27 General Assembly resolution 64/289, 2 July 2010, paragraphs 49–90.

28 The main contributors to the UN regular budget are extremely reluctant to expand the number of days programmed for intergovernmental meetings, given the high budgetary implication of each (in interpreters, officers, and logistical support). However, the other decisions contained in resolution 68/1 should lead to greater efficiency and increased productivity of each session.

29 General Assembly resolution 66/288, 27 July 2012, especially op. 84 to 86: "We decide to establish a universal, intergovernmental, high-level political forum, building on the strengths, experiences, resources and inclusive participation modalities of the Commission on Sustainable Development, and subsequently replacing the Commission."

30 General Assembly resolution 67/290, 9 July 2013, paragraphs 6 and 7.

31 General Assembly resolution 69/313, 27 July 2015, op. 132. See also General Assembly resolution 70/1, 25 September, 2016, *Transforming our world: the 2030 Agenda for Sustainable* Development, especially op. 82 to 87.

32 On 9 July 2013, the General Assembly tried, one more time, to define areas of differentiation between the two principal organs in resolution 67/289, titled "The United Nations in global economic governance." It reaffirmed in op. 4 "the central position of the General Assembly as the chief deliberative, policymaking and representative organ of the United Nations ..." and in op. 5 that the Economic and Social Council is "a principal body for policy review, policy dialogue and recommendations on issues of economic and social development and for the follow-up to the Millennium Development Goals and a central mechanism for the coordination of the United Nations system ..." The areas of overlapping persist.

5 Electoral politics at the United Nations

A contested election in 2006

- **The genesis of a candidacy**
- **The electoral process**
- **Conclusion**

One of the most visible expressions of multilateral diplomacy at the United Nations is running for vacant posts in the numerous inter-governmental bodies. The elections usually take place either in the General Assembly or in the Economic and Social Council, depending on the bodies that candidates are vying for. Member states compete for posts that range from vice-presidencies of the General Assembly (there are 21), a presidency or vice-presidency of the Assembly's six main committees, or posts in the numerous Commissions, standing commit-tees, expert bodies, and other related bodies. Significant yearly events at the General Assembly are the elections of members to the Economic and Social Council, and especially to the Security Council.

Missions in New York expend considerable time and effort in lob-bying for leadership positions for their nationals. Those positions are considered an honor and, in more practical terms, a space which pro-vides a higher profile and presumably greater leverage in the process of decision-making on substantive matters. The plum in the electoral politics is running for one of the vacancies generated every year in the Security Council; in the case of Latin America and the Caribbean, limited to one vacancy per year.[1] The elitist nature of the Council, with its limited membership of 15, and the daunting responsibilities entrus-ted to it by the Charter, make running for the Council a major endea-vor for many missions. Countries expend not only an inordinate time and effort in this undertaking, but also, in many cases, considerable resources to finance their costly—on occasion extravagant—campaigns in contested elections.

Clearly, electoral politics is an important side of multilateral diplomacy at the United Nations, which often involves swapping support between two countries seeking different posts, or the same post in different years. It is common in the daily discourse in the corridors of the United Nations to hear that country X supports country Y's candidature for the Security Council in 2017 in exchange for support of country Y to country X's candidature for the same vacancy in 2019. Occasionally, countries are lucky enough to arrange within their regional grouping to run unopposed for a vacancy (a "clean slate" in UN parlance), but frequently they must compete with other countries vying for the same post. This chapter covers one such case, which also illustrates the dynamics of electoral politics at a micro-level in one specific—and extreme—instance.

The genesis of a candidacy

Guatemala put in its bid to run for a seat in the Security Council in 2002, with the aspiration of acceding to the vacancy assigned to its regional group (Latin America and the Caribbean) for the biennium 2007–2008. Not disposing of major resources for a campaign, it further aspired to run unopposed. However, this aspiration was frustrated early on by Ecuador, and again in 2004, when Venezuela put in its own bid for the same slot. During an interlude of roughly a year, three countries were vying for the same seat, until Ecuador withdrew its candidacy, leaving the competition to Guatemala and Venezuela. The regional group only acts as a "clearing house" for candidatures and all members of a group are entitled to compete for any vacancy available.

Guatemala clearly did not have the financial resources to compete with Venezuela, but it had some solid arguments in its favor: it had never been a member of the Council, in spite of being a signatory of the Charter, and it had acquired international legitimacy after the signing of the Peace Accords at the end of 1996. On the other hand, Venezuela had some liabilities, given its controversial position on international affairs, reflected, among other aspects, in the oversized personality of President Hugo Chávez and the leadership role he was acquiring through the generous use of Venezuela's oil proceeds for international cooperation, as well as his espousal of "socialism for the twenty-first century." Accordingly, Guatemala pressed ahead with its candidacy.

It soon became public knowledge that the United States was less than enthusiastic at the prospect of having Venezuela in the Security Council, and therefore found it convenient to promote Guatemala as the viable alternative. This circumstance raised a serious dilemma, since no Latin American country wants to be perceived as a surrogate for the United States in the matter of elections at the United Nations, while, on the other hand, the support of such an important player clearly had its advantages. Be that as it may, the contest acquired a very high profile, being presented by Venezuela—insultingly for Guatemala—more as a contest between the United States (*"el Imperio"*) and Venezuela, the leader of the Bolivarian Alliance for the Peoples of Our America (ALBA).

The election process itself became legendary at the organization, having gone through 47 rounds of balloting in October 2006. The following pages narrate the complex negotiations which led to a final resolution, whereby both Guatemala and Venezuela stepped down in favor of a third country, Panama.

The electoral process

The opening shot

The main protagonists in this drama were Nicolas Maduro, foreign minister of Venezuela (and, at the time of writing, president of Venezuela); the author, who by then was foreign minister of Guatemala; John Bolton, the permanent representative of the United States; Sheikha Haya Rashed Al Khalifa (Bahrain), the President of the General Assembly; Diego Cordovez, the permanent representative of Ecuador, who held the rotating presidency of GRULAC for the month of October; Francisco Arias Cardenas, the permanent representative of Venezuela; and Jorge Skinner-Klee, the permanent representative of Guatemala. The General Assembly meeting to elect members to fill the five upcoming vacancies in the Security Council took place on 16 October 2006.

On that day, during the initial ballot, Guatemala received 109 votes against Venezuela's 76; an encouraging beginning, but 15 votes short of the two-thirds required. Three additional ballots were held that morning, with similar results (114, 116, and 110 votes for Guatemala against 74, 75, and 70 votes for Venezuela). After the lunch break, an additional five ballots were held, with the gap between both countries narrowing somewhat. The first day revealed that both countries had a "hard core" of supporters that was not willing to bend: in the case of Guatemala, some 15 votes short of a two-thirds majority; conversely, in the case of Venezuela, somewhat more than one-third, which impeded Guatemala to be elected. Under normal circumstances, a country in the situation that Venezuela found itself in would graciously concede and allow its opponent to prevail. But Venezuela refused to step down, invoking that, as a matter of national dignity, it would never make a concession of this sort to "*el Imperio.*"

As a result of this impasse, things dragged on during the 47 ballots held between 17 and 31 October, with some variations, but in each and every ballot Guatemala led Venezuela with anywhere from 20 to 37 votes (but always shy of the two-thirds majority required). In the meantime, the Latin American and Caribbean Group was getting increasingly restless, and very early on started promoting the idea that both Guatemala and Venezuela should step down in favor of a third party. The precedent invoked was a similar situation produced in 1979, when Colombia and Cuba were competing for an elected seat on the Security Council, and after 154 rounds of balloting stepped down in favor of Mexico.[2]

The idea of a consensus candidate

The reason that GRULAC members launched the idea of a "third candidate" or consensus candidate quite early is that many delegations felt uncomfortable with the spectacle unfolding in the General Assembly, which they viewed as adversely affecting the image of the Group. Further, they felt equally uncomfortable with the prospect of having to pick sides between Venezuela and Guatemala. The optics being projected by Venezuela as Guatemala being "used" by the United States to prevent their own election to the Security Council, with the insinuation that Guatemala would pay back the sole superpower by doing its bidding in the Security Council, was having some impact. At the same time many countries—within and outside of GRULAC—were equally suspicious of Venezuela's intentions should it succeed in becoming a member of the Council. A final element at play was the recollection of the battle between Colombia and Cuba in the election of 1979. In fact, on the very first day of balloting, after the fifth or sixth round, Ambassador Diego Cordovez, in his capacity as President of GRULAC, offered his good offices to bring about consultations which could lead to the third-candidate solution. He also offered to convene an "informal-informal" meeting of GRULAC to analyze the situation. This meeting was held at noon on 18 October in Conference Room 8.

During the meeting, the delegates of both Guatemala and Venezuela made presentations to GRULAC. Both indicated for differing reasons that they were not prepared to step down. Guatemala stressed that it was independently running its campaign, and firmly rejected the idea that it was a surrogate of the US. It suggested that in the light of the voting pattern that had emerged, the honorable thing for Venezuela to do was to step down so that Guatemala could claim the region's seat for the period 2007–2008. For its part, the Permanent Representative of Venezuela argued that dignity was at stake, since the United States not only had veto power over the decisions of the Security Council, but was now trying to exercise veto power on who could be elected to the Council, and Guatemala was being used as the foil. He urged all GRULAC members to reject this imposition, and even suggested that GRULAC issue a declaration to that effect. He indicated that the contest was not between two GRULAC members, but between Venezuela and the United States.

Most GRULAC members intervened in the discussion with differing positions. But all recognized the sovereign right of both Guatemala and Venezuela to persist in their respective campaigns. Not one country picked up on Venezuela's call for a declaration. The main conclusion reached was that the third-party alternative could not be imposed on Guatemala and Venezuela, and could only become an option once these two countries came to such a conclusion on their own. It also became clear during the discussion that there were considerable different viewpoints regarding which country could play the role of a consensus candidate (it appeared that each potential candidate aroused opposition among at least one other member of the Group). The additional conclusions that emerged from the meeting were, first, that the president for October, Ambassador Cordovez, should continue his good offices to Guatemala and Venezuela in the event that a solution could be found. Second, that no further meetings of the Group should be held until the two countries or the president of the Group had something specific to report. It had become clear that the matter had the risky potential of dividing the Group. Indeed, when opposing interests of two or more members of the Group were at stake, it was an article of faith for the Group to maintain strict impartiality.

The stalemate

The President of the General Assembly was also becoming concerned with the delay in concluding the elections of the new Security Council members, and held two meetings with the heads of both delegations in these initial days.

By common agreement between Guatemala and Venezuela, the balloting in the General Assembly was interrupted on 18 October, but resumed all day 19 October. The outcome of the balloting did not change much, as intense lobbying efforts continued, even on the floor of the General Assembly, with Ambassador Bolton in ubiquitous attendance.[3] At the same time, on 18 October, after the GRULAC meeting was held, Ambassador Cordovez invited the delegates of Guatemala (foreign minister and permanent representative) and Venezuela (permanent representative) to meet with him. Both sides expressed a willingness to meet, but with the caveat that neither side was prepared to step down.

The first meeting took place in the mission of Ecuador on 23 October, with the permanent representatives present. Ambassador Cordovez actively promoted the notion of a third candidate, and put forth his idea of advancing the candidature of Costa Rica, a country that aspired to the vacancy to be generated for 2008–2009. Venezuela indicated that Costa Rica would not be an acceptable alternative for his Government, but it could consider withdrawing in favor of Bolivia, under the condition that Guatemala do the same. Guatemala indicated that it was definitely not prepared to withdraw. It was also agreed that the meeting should be handled as a discreet, private initial consultation, to be followed by a new meeting at the ministerial level on 26 October. However, this agreement was soon violated, as Ambassador Cardenas of Venezuela informed the media that the meeting had taken place, that both candidates had expressed their willingness to step down, and that Venezuela had put forth the names of some countries, including Bolivia and the Dominican Republic, while Guatemala had put forth the name of Costa Rica.

The author was stunned at the news, since, as already noted, Guatemala had not offered to step down, nor had it put forth any proposals regarding consensus candidates. To make matters worse, the following day the wire services informed that President Evo Morales of Bolivia had announced that President Chávez of Venezuela had offered to promote Bolivia as a consensus candidate to replace both Venezuela and Guatemala. This of course became instant headline news in Guatemala, and prompted a flurry of calls from the press, as well as stern disclaimers from the Presidency of Guatemala. It also provoked a formal protest from Guatemala addressed to both Ambassador Cardenas and Ambassador Cordovez. The latter felt compelled to face the press to give his independent assessment of what had transpired in the meeting. In addition, Ambassador Cordovez took the initiative of convening a meeting of GRULAC to inform member states in the same terms.

This was the background of mistrust that shaped the meeting of 26 October, with both Minister Maduro and the author in attendance, together with their respective permanent representatives. From the outset, Ambassador Cordovez aggressively pushed for the third candidate solution. He arrived at the meeting with a list in hand of all potential contenders, and asked both ministers to identify those countries that could potentially be acceptable as a consensus candidate. Guatemala declined to follow this path; rather, it indicated its full commitment to persist and reiterated its judgment that the two-thirds majority to get elected was within its grasp. In addition, it pointed out that there was mounting pressure at home to pursue the candidacy.[4]

Minister Maduro, for his part, indicated that he had nothing but the highest respect for Guatemala as a nation, but that Venezuela's struggle was a principled one, against the "imposition" of one country's will on the others. Apparently, the minister saw no inconsistency in expressing respect for Guatemala and at the same time casting Guatemala as nothing but a surrogate to promote US interests. He, too, said that he was willing to persist in Venezuela's candidacy, but showed greater flexibility than Guatemala by stating that he was equally prepared to consider stepping down, on the condition that Guatemala do the same. Should this be the case, he again proposed Bolivia as a suitable consensus candidate.

Guatemala countered that it was not in a position to discuss alternative candidates while insisting on pursuing its candidacy. Nor, in the remote case that there should be a change in position, could it agree on a candidature of Bolivia, since that country did not seem to have the profile that could command broad support as a "consensus" candidate. In this regard, the unilateral announcement of Venezuela promoting Bolivia as a consensus candidate without prior consultation with Guatemala was deemed a non-starter, only made worse by President Evo Morales' unilateral announcement.

At this interlude, Diego Cordovez pushed his idea even more strenuously. He suggested that the situation in the General Assembly had stabilized, and saw no clear path for either of the candidates to garner the two-thirds majority. When Guatemala stood firm, Ambassador Cordovez, in expressing understanding for Guatemala's position, asked if said position might change in the near future. The author responded that the situation was being re-assessed every day, and of course the hypothetical possibility of a third candidate existed; Guatemala just did not see any justification to even consider such a move at the time. In consequence, the meeting was adjourned, but all parties agreed to meet again in one week in order to keep the lines of communication open. A date was set for 1 November.

The consultations get contentious

Before adjourning, there was a brief discussion regarding how the results of the meeting would be presented to the media and to other GRULAC colleagues, since there was an expectation that a consensus candidate might emerge from same, and that clearly had not occurred. Everyone agreed that Ambassador Cordovez should make a factual statement that the meeting had been friendly, that no specific agreements had been reached, but that both parties had decided to meet again within a week to continue consultations.

As the participants in the meeting were already standing and saying their goodbyes, Diego Cordovez asked what we would be talking about if the situation did not change, and why we could not at least discuss names of potential countries that would be acceptable to both Guatemala and Venezuela. Guatemala again stated that it was not prepared to take this route, although should the time come both Guatemala and Venezuela would have to agree on a country, instead of unilaterally proposing candidates, as had been the case of Venezuela's announcement regarding Bolivia.

In a more private conversation between the two of us, the author confided in him that if Guatemala became convinced that it could not gather a two-thirds majority, we might want to consider a country from the English-speaking Caribbean. I explained that there were two reasons for this. First, given the close ties between Venezuela and those countries, it would be difficult for the former to turn down a candidate from that sub-region. Second, Guatemala might want to make a good-will gesture to the CARICOM countries, which tended to view it with suspicion due to the historical territorial dispute with Belize. For this reason, beyond the immediate matter at hand, one of Guatemala's foreign policy priorities was to improve relations with the countries of the sub-region. The author was fully aware that by simply discussing this matter he was inching in the direction that Ambassador Cordovez wanted him to go, so he underlined that these were private ruminations, and of a strictly personal nature.

In spite of the agreement between the two ministers that it was Ambassador Cordovez who would brief the press on what had transpired in the meeting, that very afternoon, Minister Maduro convened the press to inform—or rather misinform—that on Monday Guatemala had indicated willingness to seek a consensus candidate, and that several names had been discussed, but that by Wednesday it had changed its position. He further ventured that this erratic behavior was no doubt due to the conflicting "instructions" being received from the

United States, and he ended up by indicating that Guatemala had cut off all future communications with Venezuela, so that the latter had no choice but to carry on its campaign.

The author again made his outrage known in writing, to both Minister Maduro and Ambassador Cordovez. For the second time in ten days Venezuela put out patently false declarations of what had transpired in private meetings, in statements that clearly did not reflect the spirit or content of what had been discussed the day before, and which further violated the agreement regarding confidentiality. Special umbrage was taken at the statement that Guatemala was under "instructions" from the United States, and the obvious contradiction was pointed out between the announcement that conversations had been broken off, when it had specifically been agreed to meet again in a week.

Minister Maduro did not respond to the author's letter. Instead, he requested meetings with all the regional groups of ambassadors (he actually secured meetings with the Arab Group and the Asian Group), to transmit the message that Venezuela was willing to step down subject to Guatemala doing the same, but that Guatemala was adamant in not doing so. On the defensive, Guatemala belatedly asked to be received by the same groups in order to clarify its own position. Further, the author was personally very disturbed at the duplicitous behavior that the minister was showing; not once, but systematically.

Transition towards an outcome

Voting resumed in the General Assembly on 31 October. The first ballot again did not reflect any significant change in relation to the previous week: Guatemala obtained 105 votes, and Venezuela 77. In other words, from the author's standpoint the good news was that Guatemala maintained its considerable lead, but the bad news was that no headway was being made in closing the gap between the actual support and the needed two-thirds majority. In the author's own mind, the time was fast approaching where the third-candidate option would have to be seriously considered.

In consequence, that very same afternoon a meeting was held in Guatemala with President Oscar Berger and Vice-President Eduardo Stein to discuss the matter, and especially the third candidate option. Should such an option be contemplated, the author proposed Barbados as a suitable candidate. It was a small country, with a strong standing in the conduct of its international affairs, which had never served in the Security Council, and which was well respected in CARICOM. The gesture would also presumably help to improve Guatemala's standing in the CARICOM community. Vice-President Stein, himself a foreign minister from 1996 to 2000, found the idea intriguing, while President Berger was dubious, but did not reject the notion outright. He did mention Panama as another plausible option, although his strong preference was to carry on the fight. The author returned to New York that evening to be present in the following day's meeting convened by Ambassador Cordovez.

The author found a new dynamic setting in upon arrival on 1 November. Venezuela's frequent protestations regarding its willingness to step down but Guatemala's insistence on continuing its campaign were having an impact; i.e., Guatemala was increasingly being viewed as the obstacle to a rapid solution to the stalemate. There were also rising expectations, promoted by several GRULAC members, that a consensus candidate would indeed be forthcoming, which could easily mitigate the incentive for countries to continue supporting Guatemala. On the other hand, a "hard core" of supporters (among them, Mexico, Colombia, and Canada, most EU countries and particularly Spain; as well as Japan, Korea and Singapore) were urging Guatemala to persist. The author went into the 1 November meeting with Minister Maduro without having taken the decision to recommend to the government to step down. Accordingly, he decided to listen to the minister first, before reacting to Ambassador Cordovez's invitation to both parties to step down and agree on a third consensus candidate.

At the start of the meeting, Minister Maduro reiterated that Venezuela was prepared to step down if Guatemala would also do so, and that, while his government continued to support Bolivia as a suitable candidate, he could be flexible in discussing other possibilities. The author began by stating that he did not have the authorization to step down, and that anything discussed this morning would have to be subject to approval from "my capital" (indeed, the Embassy of Venezuela in Guatemala had already informed Minister Maduro of President Berger's declaration, carried in that morning's local press, that Guatemala would not step down). The author also expressed surprise at Minister Maduro's declarations to the press after the last meeting. For the first time, the initiative of stepping down was mentioned as a possibility.

What followed was a conversation about hypothetical situations, since Guatemala had not agreed to desist in its candidacy. However, an additional step was taken by floating the idea of Barbados as a consensus candidate. Minister Maduro indicated that it was an interesting idea, but that he would have to consult with his superiors. Further, he ventured that perhaps it would be preferable to let the CARICOM countries select the most suitable candidate among their members. What he did not indicate, but we learned about it shortly after the meeting, is that he had met with the CARICOM caucus that very morning for breakfast, and had indicated that Venezuela would try to persuade Guatemala to support a CARICOM country as a consensus candidate, and that he felt that it should be left up to CARICOM to select the most suitable country.

The author's immediate reaction was to express that it was not a good idea to put the burden of picking a specific country on CAR-ICOM. Firstly, because it would plant a seed of discord within the group, which he considered an unnecessary obligation. In the second place, because, should the idea of a third candidate take hold, it was really up to Guatemala and Venezuela to come up with a proposal, which would then have to be submitted to the consideration of GRULAC. The author asked Minister Maduro directly if, under a hypothetical scenario, he could support Barbados, but no direct answer was forthcoming. Rather, Minister Maduro retreated to the reiteration of Bolivia or "other countries of the region" as alternatives. Clearly there was resistance on his part regarding the suggestion of Barbados.

The author felt that he was being drawn into a tacit acceptance of selecting a third candidate, when he had express instructions not to do. At his request, the meeting was adjourned for the morning, among other aspects so that both parties could consult with their respective capitals. In fact, the author did call Vice-President Stein to tell him that he was beginning to lean in the direction of accepting the consensus candidate argument in order to avoid a protracted and probably debilitating campaign. He had already spent three weeks in New York (with two brief trips for consultations), and other pressing matters were looming back home. He also proposed that, should Guatemala step down, a strong case could be made to GRULAC to allow an unopposed candidacy at the first available date (which turned out to be the elections of 2011). Vice-President Stein was sympathetic with these reflections and also with the idea of supporting Barbados as a consensus candidate, and indicated that he would discuss it with President Berger. Less than an hour later, he called back indicating President Berger's position, which included a reluctant acceptance of a third-party candidate, reluctant support for Barbados as the consensus country, and a reiteration that, should the occasion arise, he would prefer Panama as a consensus candidate.

Things were moving fast enough now to consider whether Barbados would even be willing or able to accept being the consensus candidate, so the author took the opportunity of the lunch break to raise this possibility with Ambassador Christopher Hackett of Barbados, who suggested that a weighty matter of this nature should be taken up with his foreign minister. Accordingly, the author took the step of calling Dame Billie Miller, foreign minister of Barbados. She was, of course, surprised at the inquiry, and indicated that she would have to reflect on the matter and to discuss it with her prime minister. The author indicated that he just wanted to give her a "heads up" in case such a scenario could materialize, and that he felt compelled to share with her his own thinking on the matter. The conversation ended on a slightly upbeat note, in that the minister reiterated that it was an interesting notion and that she by no means could rule it out, but simply needed some time to process it and provide a reaction.

The outcome

As the afternoon session began, the author indicated that his president was not convinced that we should step down, but that he had the authorization to sound out different options of a consensus candidate prior to taking a firm decision. In this context, he indicated that Guatemala's first choice would be Barbados, for the reasons expressed in the off-the-cuff conversation of 26 October with Ambassador Cordovez. No mention was made of the lunch-time conversation with Foreign Minister Miller. Minister Maduro did not reject the idea of Barbados, but stuck to the argument that it was up to the CARICOM countries to select a candidate from their group. He also indicated that Venezuela could agree to a few Latin American countries, including Panama. Guatemala countered that the selection of a candidate could not be left to a sub-regional block.

It was around this procedural disagreement that, when Guatemala finally gave in to the idea of stepping down in favor of a third party, it was Panama that emerged as the potential consensus candidate. The author was secure in the knowledge that President Berger had expressed a preference for that country, while Venezuela had actually put forward the name of Panama.

Prior to reaching the agreement, both ministers consulted with their respective presidents, and then with President Martin Torrijos of Panama, who almost instantly gave his consent. But these agreements had coalesced after the meeting had concluded. Before leaving the Mission of Ecuador, it was decided that Ambassador Cordovez would make a brief statement to the press that we had had a useful and productive consultation, that some progress was made, and that we had agreed to continue the discussion in the late afternoon (the appointed hour was at 5 p.m.).

The deputy permanent representative of Ecuador called both parties by phone about one hour after the meeting had been adjourned, to indicate that Venezuela had accepted Panama as a potential consensus candidate. Subsequently, Guatemala confirmed its acceptance of stepping down in favor of Panama as a consensus candidate. This decision was not taken lightly, but it appeared to be the most realistic option, given the results of the voting in the previous day's ballots, as well as the unhelpful attitude of some South American GRULAC members who clearly wanted to put these protracted negotiations behind them. So, by five in the afternoon, when the meeting was resumed, two of the three most important decisions had already been taken: first, Guatemala and Venezuela would step down; second, both countries, Guatemala and Venezuela, had agreed to propose Panama to GRULAC as a consensus candidate. The third decision that could not be resolved without additional consultation was the acquiescence of Panama to accept a role as a consensus candidate, but, as stated, the acceptance was received shortly thereafter. That seemed to be the end of the road for Guatemala's initiative on Barbados. Arrangements were hastily made, in consultation with El Salvador (which assumed the Presidency of GRULAC on 1 November) to convene the Group on the following day, 2 November.

At around 7:30 p.m. Ambassador Cordovez triumphantly convened the press (numerous journalists were waiting in the corridors) to announce the decision. Both Minister Maduro and the author gave brief statements confirming the remarks of Ambassador Cordovez. It was not a happy moment for Guatemala, since the considerable work and energy spent on a one-year campaign was capitalized in literally an instant by another country that had not even entertained the thought of becoming a member of the Security Council. However, those are subjective matters that do not belong in this narrative.

The GRULAC meeting took place on 2 November, at noon. Ambassador Cordovez made some brief remarks to explain what had happened in the prior consultations between himself and the two foreign ministers, under his presidency of GLULAC. Minister Maduro made a brief presentation, reiterating his Government's acceptance of Panama as a consensus candidate, and with an indirect dig against Guatemala, his satisfaction that Venezuela's position of both candidates having to step down had prevailed, which he viewed as a victory against the United States. The author made a statement lamenting the refusal of Venezuela to step down, in spite of Guatemala's clear numerical advantage in the balloting, and, importantly, announced that Guatemala had already notified the new President of GRULAC,

El Salvador, of its candidacy for the Security Council for the next slot available, which was for the biennium 2012–2013. He expressed the hope that, in the light of the events of the last month, GRULAC member states would allow Guatemala to run unopposed in the elections to be held in October 2011; i.e., five years from the date.

There was the expectation that GRULAC would approve the consensus candidacy of Panama without further discussion, but the CARICOM countries asked for time to consult with their respective governments. It turned out that they had been led to believe in the meeting held previously with Minister Maduro that a member of CARICOM would become a consensus candidate, and that they had only learned through the media that Panama had been the anointed country. It appears that Minister Maduro did not take the precaution of informing the CARICOM caucus on the results of the ensuing discussion in the Ecuadorian Mission (the author did inform the permanent representative of Barbados on the matter right after the press conference of the previous evening). The GRULAC meeting was adjourned until the following day. The author returned to Guatemala that afternoon, and only learned the next day, on 3 November, that GRULAC had unanimously endorsed the candidacy of Panama, which was finally ratified by the General Assembly on 7 November with 164 member states voting in favor.

Conclusion

The aforementioned narrative covers an unusual event, in greater than usual detail. It is conveyed to illustrate the many twists and turns countries endure in steering their candidacies for posts in the United Nations: in this instance, for an elected seat in the Security Council. As stated, the internal candidacies for such posts are also an important element of multilateral diplomacy at the United Nations, and occasionally become overriding obsessions of some of the ambassadors charged with seeking successful outcomes to their aspirations.

As a coda to this narrative, GRULAC respected the request to let Guatemala run unopposed in 2011. In fact, two countries, Argentina and Chile, postponed their candidacies by one year each in order to be allowed to run unopposed themselves in 2012 and 2013, respectively. Further, the GRULAC's last contested election took place in 2007 (Costa Rica was elected in its contest against the Dominican Republic), and since that time only uncontested elections have taken place. This is due in no small measure to the events that took place in 2006, described above and their traumatic aftermath on GRULAC. Finally, as mentioned in the following chapter, Guatemala was elected to the Security Council for a two-year term on 17 October 2011 by unanimity among the 190 votes cast; an indisputable vindication of the frustrated campaign that took place five years earlier.

Notes

1 As is well known, there are ten elected members of the Security Council for two year, non- renewable terms. Two of these posts are allocated to GRULAC by General Assembly resolution 1991 (XVIII), 17 December 1993, paragraph 3.
2 The narrative that follows draws heavily on the author's minutes. Unfortunately, Ambassador Diego Cordovez, who was deeply involved in the consultations, passed away in May 2014. Presumably his own notes are still on file in the mission of Ecuador to the United Nations.
3 In his book Ambassador John R. Bolton, then permanent representative of the United States to the United Nations gives his own version of the described events. See: John R. Bolton, *Surrender is not an Option: Defending America at the United Nations* (New York: Threshold Edition, 2007), 263–272.
4 The Guatemalan Congress had approved a Resolution on 25 October (an unprecedented act) urging the Executive Branch to vigorously pursue the candidature.

6 The Security Council in 2012–2013

The perspective of small states

- **The unique perspective of small states**
- **Induction of new members**
- **The two-tier governance structure**
- **Some particularly divisive issues**
- **The main point of tension**
- **Other aspects of the system of governance**
- **Organizational questions**
- **On the matter of transparency**
- **Relations with other principal organs**
- **On the legitimacy of the Security Council**
- **Security Council reform**
- **Conclusion**

There are 188 member states of the United Nations that can potentially be elected to serve in the Security Council (in contrast to the five member states that are permanent members). They are a very heterogeneous group of countries. Some are very large and proactive on the world stage, and a few even feel that they have every right to the same privileges that permanent members have. On the other side of the spectrum, there are numerous small countries whose relative weight on the world stage is negligible, and then there are a sizeable number of states that fit somewhere in-between. There appears to be some correlation—understandable and justifiable—between the size and influence of states and the number of times they have served on the Security Council. For example, Brazil, Colombia, and Guatemala were all founding members of the United Nations, but by 2012 Brazil had served ten times and Colombia seven, while Guatemala only joined the Council for the first time in that year.

Most of those 188 member states share varying degrees of frustration and dissatisfaction with the Security Council, and the bulk of these feelings gravitate around the separation between permanent and elected members, defying the principle enunciated in Article 2 (1) of the Charter regarding the sovereign equality of all states. Not only are five countries accorded the privilege or permanency to an organ that others must aggressively compete for to fill one of its vacancies, but the latter bridle at the *de facto* weighted voting system bestowed by Article 27 (3) of the Charter, whereby five countries' vote in selected cases carries infinite weight, while the other ten countries' vote corresponds to the principle of equality among states. In addition, 188 countries are compelled to comply with the Security Council's decision taken under Chapter VII, while five have an escape route—the use of the veto—which offers liberation from compliance by impeding the resolution in the first place.

Other sources of frustration revolve around opaque working methods, the exceptional privileges that permanent members bestow on themselves by tightly controlling most aspects of the Council's work, and even the content of information on its work provided to the public at large; the fact that the current permanent members reflect the world of 1945, rather than the word of today; real or alleged encroachment of the Security Council into the purview of the other principal organs, as well as the exceptional powers assigned to the Security Council, which in their scope far exceed the power assigned to the General Assembly. Even the elitist nature of an organ of 15 members "acting on the behalf" of the full membership (Article 24 (1)) rankles the vast majority, adding fuel to the continuous demands for "reform" of the Council, including its expansion. This topic has been at the top of the General Assembly's agenda for decades, with relatively little progress to show for it, except perhaps in having achieved greater transparency regarding working methods and access to information concerning the Council's activities.

In spite of all these sources of discontent, most member states seem to be keen to join the Council,[1] and, as mentioned in the previous chapter, many go to great lengths to realize this aspiration. After the frustrated attempt to join this Organ in 2006 (Chapter 6), Guatemala finally took its seat on 1 January, 2012. The author had the privilege of representing the country during its two-year tenure. This gave him the opportunity to observe the functioning of the Council as a full member, palpating its dynamics from "inside the beast."

This chapter deliberately avoids narrating Guatemala's experience, how it navigated the multifaceted agenda of the Council and its subsidiary bodies, the positions it took regarding the different agenda items at the time, and its pet issues (among others, the situation in Haiti, over which Guatemala, as one of the two Latin American members of the Council, assumed a special sense of ownership).[2]

Rather, the accent in the pages that follow is on issues of greater universal significance revolving around the Security Council, as perceived by an "insider" from a relatively small country (under 17 million inhabitants) with fairly weak credentials on the world stage.

The latter explains the somewhat unconventional organization of the different topics explored in the following pages. And even those topics are very selective, since the enormous breadth of the Council's activities and working methods gives rise to an infinite number of subjects, which opens the possibility of lengthy, broad and detailed treatment.[3] This narrative is, of course, not unique, but other recent attempts to describe what life was like as a member of the Council refer to more advanced and larger countries.[4] At any rate, it is safe to say that for anyone interested in multilateral diplomacy, the Security Council is an unparalleled observatory.

The unique perspective of small states

The Charter establishes in Article 23 (1) two requisites to be elected to the Security Council: first, that "due regard ... be specially paid, in the first instance to the contribution of Members of the United Nations to the maintenance of international peace and security and to the other purposes of the Organization ..." and, second, that there should be "equitable geographical distribution." The first requisite is, of course, open to interpretation, but over the years the bar as to which countries "contribute to the maintenance of international peace and security" has come down, especially as many of them joined the ranks of the troop and police contributors, while fitting into the category of "and other purposes of the Organization" is even more vague, opening the door for virtually all members to consider themselves eligible. The second requisite was rapidly resolved in the context of the wider membership's division into five regional geographical blocks, mostly for electoral purposes.[5]

The reasons for small countries wanting to join the Council are varied, and, in many cases, of a singular nature. At one level, it reflects the core belief that one of the many benefits of multilateralism is precisely that of giving smaller countries a voice and the possibility of participating in global decisions, in contrast to an alternative world which could be dominated by unilateralism. In other words, participating in the Security Council is, among other aspects, a validation of all that is positive about multilateral diplomacy. At another level, for smaller countries, being a member of the Council tends to be viewed as a matter of prestige and recognition. Certainly that was the case for

Guatemala, which emerged from a four-decade long internal conflict in 1996 with the signing of peace accords, thus breaking a long period of international isolation. By presenting itself as a modern, democratic, rule of law-abiding, as well as a forward looking state, joining the Security Council was the culmination of a deliberate policy begun in 1996, and pursued by all successive governments, of achieving full acceptance on the global stage. Smaller countries also like to argue that their presence is beneficial to the Council's work, by diversifying the points of view on any given agenda item and contributing, even modestly, to the "democratization" of the organ. Small countries can also influence in shaping the Council's agenda, especially during their presidency and through the chairmanship of any subsidiary bodies they are charged with.

At the same time, there are some obvious downsides to joining the Council; in general, but especially for smaller countries. These include the financial implications of campaigning and then of maintaining a large enough mission in New York to play a responsible role, a desire not to compromise bilateral relations with possible conflicts associated with taking sides on contentious issues debated in the multilateral arena, and possible opposition on the part of domestic public opinion that often fails to see any advantages and might perceive disadvantages in such a venture. There also is a concern on the capacity of small countries to navigate the rough waters of an organ dominated by the major world powers. Finally, there are a few countries—not necessarily limited to their size or relative weight in international affairs—that do not desire to join the Council as elected members on matters of principle, since they object to its system of governance.[6]

With the benefit of hindsight, what can be said with certainty is that in Guatemala's case the two years as members of the Security Council were a cornucopia of learning, resulting in the professionalization of its foreign service, especially in terms of negotiations and the enhancement of skills on multilateral affairs. There was a wide array of topics where important insights were assimilated, both on process—working methods, rules of procedure, how the Council and the secretariat interact—as well as on specific country-based and issues-based matters. The Council can be considered the major league of multilateral diplomacy, since the stakes often are high and the negotiations taking place are usually very intense. On occasion, hard ball diplomacy is practiced, as occurred in 2003 when the United States tried to persuade several of its bilateral partners—including other permanent members such as China, France, and the Russian Federation—to support a resolution authorizing the use of "all necessary means" to obligate the Government of Iraq to eliminate its arsenal of weapons of mass destruction (nonexistent, as it later turned out).[7] However, during the author's experience, the *démarches* received on various issues, at UN Headquarters and in the capital, were always respectful and devoid of anything suggesting adverse consequences should the particular matter in question not receive the requested support; a matter to be revisited below.

The author also believes that, in spite of its limited space on the world stage, as occurs with many smaller countries, Guatemala made a significant contribution to the work of the Council during its tenure. To do so, it adopted early on a simple, two-pronged strategy. First, it prepared itself in order to present informed and coherent positions on the matters under consideration, as reflected in statements in formal and informal sessions and especially in the quiet and painstaking participation in drafting outcome documents—resolutions, presidential statements, press statements, and *communiqués*—when these were negotiated, paragraph by paragraph, line by line, and word by word. Second, it specialized in a specific topic, born out of its own experience during its internal conflict, which consisted of putting special emphasis on all matters related to the rule of law and its link to peace and justice. Indeed, the promotion and defense of the rule of law became the "brand" of the Guatemalan delegation.[8] The topic selected for the open debate of Guatemala's presidency of the Security Council was "Peace and justice, with a special focus on the role of the International Criminal Court."[9] In that same vein, one of the subsidiary bodies entrusted to Guatemala (in addition to the 1572 Sanctions Committee on Côte d'Ivoire) was the Informal Working Group on International Tribunals,[10] which dealt with the Tribunals of ex-Yugoslavia and Rwanda.[11] In summary, the only point to be made here is that smaller countries, if well organized, can indeed benefit from participating in the work of the Security Council and, of equal importance, contribute in a significant manner to its work.[12]

Induction of new members

Countries that aspire to be elected to the Security Council tend to take their responsibility seriously. They usually prepare for the occasion months ahead of their election (and more intensely after being elected but before assuming their seat on the Council),[13] by consulting with colleagues that have undergone the experience previously, reading up on issues and procedures, training and strengthening their staffs as well as distributing specific assignments to their specialists.[14] They are also invited to sit in as observers of the work of the Council and all its subsidiary bodies during the last six weeks of the year.[15] Further, the Government of Finland had generously sponsored since 2002 a two-day full immersion seminar for new members aptly called "Hitting the Ground Running." UNITAR also offered some training to staff of newly elected missions, albeit of a less rigorous content. It is customary for each of the elected members to head at least two subsidiary bodies (usually a sanctions committee, an *ad hoc* body, or a working group), and often it is informed of the responsibilities it will assume before taking up its duties so that it can adequately prepare itself.[16] As already noted, presiding over a sanctions committee is one of the many ways in which small countries can help shape Security Council policies.[17] In short, by the time a newly elected country takes its seat, it has at least a strong inkling of what is awaiting it.

When the aspiration of joining the Security Council is finally fulfilled, the elected country, especially if it is joining for the first time, often tends to undergo an instant transformation from a vocal critic of everything about the Security Council to at the very least displaying a more tolerant attitude towards its real or perceived flaws. It is difficult to surmise whether this change of attitude is due to the heady and adrenaline-high atmosphere of having finally acceded to this elite forum, or whether it is traceable to a deliberate process of cooptation on the part of the P5 that takes place from the very first moment. The author, who had frequently criticized this somewhat hypocritical syndrome in other colleagues, was surprised to recognize it in his own changing attitude as he assumed his seat at the iconic table of the Security Council on 1 January, 2012.

This instant feeling of belonging to "something special" is probably not accidental. As Kishore Mahbubani noted when he led the delegation of Singapore as a first-time elected member in 2001–2002:

> in the two years that I served on the Council, I could not point to a specific instance where the elected members were treated disrespectfully or as second-class citizens by the P-5. We spent most of our time in closed-door informal consultations, conducted in a small chamber ... relationships at a personal level were marked by a warm senses of camaraderie, which is often generated by working together in close quarters over an extended period of time.[18]

Having said the above, most of the rest of Ambassador Mahbubani's article revolves around the abyss that divides the P5 from the E10 and his perception that the elected members are being somehow manipulated by the permanent members, to the point that he describes the P-5 in terms of their "believing that they 'own' the Council."[19]

The two-tier governance structure

Like Ambassador Mahbubani, the author also felt that he was invariably treated with respect and that the members of his team were always accorded their place. At the same time, the cleavage between the two categories of members was more than obvious; in fact, it was the defining trait of the Council. In addition to the lopsided characteristics between permanent and elected members alluded to above, the P5 included some of the most important actors on the world stage, given their size, their economic and financial weight, their cultural influence, and, above all, their military might. This fact alone set them apart in the pecking order of an organization where all countries are only equal in a formal sense (the principle of "sovereign equality"), while everyone understands, as noted in Chapter 3, that "some are more equal than others."

Permanence also comes hand in hand with global interests, institutional memory, copious experience on everything from rules of procedure to the situation on the ground in countries on the agenda, as well as the power of initiating and controlling actions on the part of the Council. In addition, the P5 were backed by a very wide network of diplomatic missions all over the world that were primary sources of information and analysis. In contrast, Guatemala was virtually absent from the African Continent, Central Europe, and much of South-East Asia as well as the Middle East, leaving it to access only secondary sources of information and analysis. To top it off, there was a discernible difference in attitudes: delegates from P5 countries tended to present themselves as old hands, comfortable in their skins, while the newly-arrived elected members' delegates projected the excitement of being able to join an exclusive club. Admittedly, this initial enthusiasm wore off rather quickly as the new delegates settled in, but they nevertheless continued to feel an air of arrogance on the part of members of the P5 delegations that never seemed to fully dissipate.

Various elected members seem to handle these asymmetries better than others. Some tended to harbor a greater level of resentment at the situation they found themselves in, while others seemed to grudgingly accept the rules set up in the Charter, regardless of whether they agreed or disagreed with the existing order, and tried to make the best of it. Most of the author's colleagues, and the author himself, fell somewhere in-between these extremes, on different points of the spectrum and even with differing attitudes over time, depending on the topic at hand and also on changing circumstances. But all of them pushed back frequently at the will of one or more permanent members, sometimes (rarely) by voting abstention or even against a specific initiative, and quite often by raising objections in the consultation phase and by trying to influence on the precise language of resolutions or statements. However, there seemed to be clear limits on pushing back. Those limits were shaped by a realistic assessment on the part of elected members on how far they could go in staking out an independent position in an organ where decision-making and the voting system are heavily skewed in favor of the permanent members, given existing realities, the rules of procedure, customs, and the corporate culture set in place.

One of the numerous examples in the author's experience that come to mind involves the concept of peace enforcement. Guatemala had difficulty with the decision to deploy a dedicated intervention brigade to be established within MONUSCO in March 2013, since it felt that it compromised the principles of neutrality and impartiality so essential to the spirit of peacekeeping. After mulling over whether to abstain, it ended up joining the consensus in adopting resolution 2098 (2013), but made its concerns known in a statement explaining its vote, expressing, among other aspects:

> We wish to place on record some of our concerns—concerns that caused us to waver in joining the consensus and that have not yet been fully dissipated—with regard to the resolution just adopted …
> First, we still have serious difficulties in terms of the involvement of the United Nations in peace-enforcement activities, as such activities may compromise the neutrality and impartiality that we deem so essential to the Organization's peacekeeping activities. As a matter of principle, we believe that, when domestic armed groups challenge the host-country State, the United Nations mission must offer its good offices, mediate and even take a proactive stance in resolving the dispute. But its presence should be perceived by all parties as that of an honest broker, not a potential party to the conflict … We are concerned that the entire MONUSCO runs the risk of indirectly becoming a peace enforcement mission. That would raise many conceptual, operational and legal considerations that, in our view, have not been adequately explored in the course of negotiating the text.[20]

A further layer conditioning the complex engagement between permanent and elected members and within each of the two groupings (P5 and E10) is related to the personalities involved and the policies that their governments espouse at any given time. Personalities matter, especially in multilateral settings, where networking is an essential element of consensus building. The degree of empathy and rapport that can be developed between delegates can go a long way in defining the final outcome of complex negotiations. This holds especially true for the personal interaction between representatives of E10 countries and those of P5 countries; informal conversations among members are replete with references to individual ambassadors whose passage through the Council is remembered with warm affection (for example, Jeremy Greenstock of the UK, who served from 1998 to 2003) or somewhat less than affection (for example, John Bolton of the US, who served from August 2005 to December 2006).

When exploring the dynamics between permanent and elected members, it should be clear that the P5 do not always act as a homogeneous block, any more than the elected members do. Moreover, their collective interaction in relation to the elected members varies over time.[21] The author arrived at the Council with the pre-conception that most decisions were taken first by the P5 and then brought to the attention of the elected members. Once familiarized with the *modus operandi* of the Council, that pre-conception, while not entirely erroneous in most cases, required a more nuanced understanding. To a large degree, the main core of decision-making does occur in informal consultations between the permanent members even before meetings of the whole are held, but, at least during the biennium 2012–2013, those decisions were generally not thrust on the rest of the members on a "take-it-or-leave-it" basis. Normally, enough "wiggle-room" was left in the codification of the core decisions into resolutions or presidential statements so as to give all members of the Council the opportunity to offer their inputs, and therefore achieve something akin to a sense of ownership of a collective decision; albeit, often with some reservations. In numerous cases, the changes introduced to original texts went way beyond editorial drafting, delving significantly into the substance of the matter at hand.

Of course, if elected members perceive cracks in the unity of permanent members, they try to exploit the situation by widening the "wiggle-room." But the same argument also works conversely, when divisions among elected members can be taken advantage of by one or more of the permanent members. These are merely additional examples of the infinite number or elements that go into the dynamics of engagement among the 15 members of the Security Council.

An additional general observation from the author's perspective can be made about the closed informal meetings held among the P5. In an organ that is famously characterized as opaque for non-members, probably the least transparent aspect of all, even for elected members, is the lack of knowledge of what transpires during the informal meetings of the P5. While occasionally a casual remark of one of the permanent representatives of a P5 country to one of his elected member colleagues offers a glimpse into these restricted discussions, most of the detailed content of those conversations is rarely divulged. In addition, it is fair to assume that there is a good deal of information-sharing going on among the P5—information that is not always made fully available to the E10—and in an organization where access to information is highly valued, this becomes another area of differentiation between the P5 and the E10.

It should be noted that the gatherings mentioned above are not "secret," since they often take place in a meeting rooms near the Security Council chamber, "in plain sight" of all delegations. As already noted, what emerges from these informal consultations among the P5 leads to concrete initiatives which shape the work of the Council, and that tend to put elected members at a disadvantage from the very outset.

On the other hand, when the P5 are unable to come to the elected members with a unified proposal, it is equally predictable that action will be blocked, mostly without the need for one of the parties in question to exercise the veto. The paradigm of the latter is found in the relatively few—but, since 2014, growing—instances in which the United States and the Russian Federation are unable or unwilling to find common ground, a matter that is explored in greater detail below.

Finally, in examining the dynamics between the permanent and elected members, there are a series of major tensions which are systemic in nature (i.e., not limited to the Security Council), but that tend to accentuate the cleavages that already exist within the Council. Among these, five major sets of issues are noteworthy, and all of them come into play as permanent and non-permanent members of the Council interact.

The first derives from the reluctance on the part of the P5 countries, with varying degrees of emphasis between them, to share in any way, shape, or form the responsibility of maintaining international peace and security with the other principal organs of the United Nations, in spite of the small window left ajar for the General Assembly in Article 11 (promptly mitigated by Article 12 (1)) as well as the existence of the oft quoted but rarely applied "Uniting for Peace" resolution.[22]

This issue is especially relevant in the area of peacebuilding, where attacking the root causes of conflict can partially fall under the purview of the Security Council, the General Assembly, or the Economic and Social Council. In the past, there has been little cooperation between the principal organs or even their subsidiary bodies in addressing peacebuilding (or "sustainable peace" in the most recent usage of the term).[23] In fact, since the creation of the Peacebuilding Commission in 2005, and until quite recently, some permanent members of the Security Council have shown reluctance to even invite the president of the PBC to brief them in relevant open debates, while most elected members have encouraged it.

The second source of tension is derived from the differing positions between the main contributors to the United Nations budget and the main troop and police contributors to peacekeeping operations. Although this tension plays out more in the General Assembly, both in the Special Committee on Peacekeeping Operations and in the fifth committee, it is also felt in the Security Council, since some of the elected members invariably are troop contributors, while the P5 include some of the main contributors to the UN budget. This matter came up on several occasions during the author's tenure in the Council and helped shape differing positions between both sets of members.

The third issue is derived from chapter VIII of the Charter: partnering with regional organizations. The presence of the African Union, as well as sub-regional organizations such as the Economic Community of West African States (ECOWAS), the Southern African Development Community (SADC), and the Intergovernmental Authority on Development (IGAD), has been growing over time, but the modalities of those partnerships are still a constant source of irritation, especially around who assumes the leading role, and who puts up the bulk of the financing. Some permanent members of the Security Council insist that they represent the only multilateral body that has the authority to maintain international peace and security, while some elected members (especially from the African Group) and the African Union argue that the latter is best placed to lead when it comes to conflicts in Africa. In spite of the growing importance of the African Union in peace operations on the African Continent, and especially in Somalia, Darfur, South Sudan, and Mali, the Security Council is reluctant to share the peacekeeping operations budget of the United Nations with outside bodies without exercising control on the use of funding; African troop contributors, often supported by some of the elected members to the Security Council, argue that they supply the manpower, and the least that the United Nations can do it to supply the funding. During 2012–2013, those tensions were evident in meetings of the Security Council, and also surfaced when the Security Council held its annual meetings with the Peace and Security Council (PSC) of the African Union. Something similar occurred, with a much lower scope and intensity, in the relations between the Security Council and the League of Arab States, as well as with the Gulf Cooperation Council.

The fourth issue refers to the allocation of resources and efforts between the different "pillars" of the United Nations, with the G77 demanding more resources for development as its members perceive a burgeoning peacekeeping budget—as well as rapidly growing demands for Special Political Missions—emanating from the Council, and especially the P5. The apprehension is that peace operations and, as of late, humanitarian assistance to war-torn societies are "crowding out" the organization's activities to foster development. This cleavage is also reflected in relations between the P5 and the E10.

Fifth, and very importantly, most elected members tend to prefer preventive diplomacy and the application of Chapter VI decisions, and perceive that some or all of the permanent members are too quick in calling for peacekeeping contingents and chapter VII decisions for many of the conflict situations which come to the Security Council's attention. Constant calls are made to put more emphasis on conflict prevention, which, it is held, could preclude the need for complex and expensive peacekeeping operations.

Some particularly divisive issues

But of course the main source of friction occurs at the level of agenda items, where the cleavage usually is not between permanent and elected members, but between the permanent members themselves. It should be recalled that around 90 percent of resolutions of the Council are adopted by unanimity, but among the remaining 10 percent or so there are some highly contentious issues which tend to divide and even polarize; usually—but not always—with the United States and the Russian Federation—sometimes joined by China—taking opposing positions.[24]

To illustrate, four examples come to mind. The first one gravitates around the long-standing agenda item entitled "The Situation in the Middle East including the Palestinian Question." The Council re-visits this topic every month; every third month in an open public session. It has become highly contentious, with Israel feeling increasingly isolated in the United Nations and ever more dependent on the continued support of the United States and, to a lesser degree, a few member states of the Western European and Others Group (WEOG). In the rare instances that the US uses the veto, it usually is related to this matter. For example, on 18 February 2011, 80 countries co-sponsored draft resolution S/2011/24 calling on Israel to withdraw its settlements on the West Bank.[25] The resolution received 14 votes in favor, but the

United States voted against it, arguing that the only way to reach agreement between Israel and the Palestinian Authority was through direct negotiations, and that the draft resolution only led to hardening positions, making negotiations even more difficult.[26]

A second high-profile example is found in the adoption of resolutions 1970 of 26 February and especially 1973 of 17 March 2011 regarding the rapidly deteriorating situation in Libya. The latter resolution contemplated a ceasefire with the mediation of the African Union, the further strengthening of sanctions, the imposition of a no-fly zone, and, most importantly, authorization to take "all necessary measures" to protect the civilian population of Libya, which, it was held by the sponsors of the resolution, was being seriously threatened at the time as Muammar Gaddafi responded brutally to the rebellion whose epicenter was in Benghazi. During the shaping of resolution 1973, and due to intense lobbying on the part of France and the United Kingdom, joined belatedly by the United States (as well as Lebanon, a member of the Security Council representing the Arab League), both the Russian Federation and China were prevailed upon not to use their veto power, so both countries joined Germany, Brazil, and India in voting abstention.[27] So, in contrast to resolution 1970, adopted by unanimous vote three weeks earlier, resolution 1973 was adopted with 10 votes in favor, and the 5 above-mentioned abstentions.[28] Subsequent events in Libya, and the accusation that the resolution had been designed all along to bring about a regime change, considerably poisoned the environment in which the Council worked in 2012 and beyond.[29]

That certainly was one of the factors that impacted on the third example, which refers to the tragic consequence of the failed attempts on the part of the Council during 2012 and in subsequent years to stop the bloodshed in Syria. Those failed attempts, which included joint efforts on the part of the United Nations and the League of Arab States to broker a political transition, as illustrated by the Six-Point Proposal of their Joint Special Envoy, Kofi Annan, supported unanimously by the Security Council in resolution 2042 of 14 April 2012, and, again, the renewed effort of the so-called Action Group for Syria through the *Final Communiqué* issued on 30 June 2012 in Geneva.[30] But those efforts failed, in no small part due to profound divisions within the Council, especially between the "Western members" of the P5 on the one hand, and the Russian Federation and China, on the other, all of which led to the resignation of Kofi Annan in early August 2012. His successor, Lakhdar Brahimi, only exercised these functions for 18 months before following the same course.[31]

One of the central issues which divided the permanent members then, and which persisted in 2016, revolves around the person of Bashar al-Assad, the President of Syria, with the United States and other like-minded countries arguing for his relinquishing power as part of any political solution, and the Russian Federation, sustaining that no political solution is possible without his active participation. The latter's position no doubt reflects not only Russia's historical strategic interests in Syria, but also has been influenced by the events in 2011 that led to the adoption of resolution 1973 in Libya and its subsequent consequences,

In fact, during the author's tenure in the Security Council, the veto was only invoked on two occasions, and both referred to Syria.[32] In the first instance, draft resolution S/2012/77 of 4 February 2012 received 13 votes in favor, while the Russian Federation and China voted against it, arguing that it was unbalanced in demanding compliance from the Government of Syria while hardly mentioning the armed opposition.[33] In the second instance, draft resolution S/2012/538 of 19 July 2012 again received 13 votes in favor, with the Russian Federation and China voting against, holding this time that by invoking Chapter VII of the Charter the way would be opened for sanctions and even external military involvement, much as had transpired in Libya.[34]

It is very likely that, had the Russian Federation and what was branded in their explanation of vote as "the Western members of the Security Council" reached an agreement to address the Syrian situation at the time, Syria—and the world—would have been spared the horrors that followed, and that still continue in 2016. But that was not to be: by early 2012 the Syrian rebels were already receiving open assistance, especially in armament, from some of the Gulf States and more covert assistance from Saudi Arabia and some Western powers, while the Assad regime was receiving support, both covert and overt, from the Russian Federation and the Islamic Republic of Iran. It appeared that the main external actors, instead of joining forces to extinguish the flames, were simply adding fuel to the fire.

The only area where unanimous agreement was reached regarding Syria constitutes the exception to prove the rule. In September 2013, the United States and the Russian Federation were able to find common ground on the need to destroy the Syrian Arab Republic's chemical weapons program, which led to the Council's unanimous adoption of resolution 2118 (2013).[35]

The fourth example is found in the Russian Federation's annexation of Crimea in late February 2014, violating, according to most observers, the principle of territorial integrity of Ukraine, and which left

Russia quite isolated within the Council, notwithstanding its arguments to justify its actions. These were based both on a historical justification and the more immediate request of the Supreme Council of Crimea, which acted in accordance with the results of the alleged overwhelming results of a referendum held days before. On 15 March 2014, the United States tabled draft resolution S/2014/189 condemning the act and put it to a vote, with 13 countries in favor, China abstaining, and the Russian Federation voting against; i.e., applying a veto.[36]

The main point of tension

The larger point to be made is that in spite of the fact that 90 percent of the resolutions of the Council are adopted unanimously, it is the other 10 percent that include the more notorious conflicts in the world, which increasingly lead to the criticism regarding the ineffectiveness of the Security Council (and, by extension of the United Nations). In fact, the inability of the Permanent Members to agree on sustainable political settlements in Syria, Libya, South Sudan, Darfur, and Mali during the author's tenure in the Council proved to have catastrophic consequences in terms of human suffering in all cases.

In the matter of Syria, by 2014–2015, those consequences spilled over in predictable ways, provoking death and indescribable suffering for hundreds of thousands of people, providing added fuel to radical Jihadist groups, and provoking mass migrations of refugees, including into Western Europe. Old conflicts—the Israeli-Palestinian situation and the Western Sahara—continued to fester, while new ones—Yemen and the emerging situation in Ukraine—burst onto the scene. These dysfunctional patterns are of course perceptible to the elected members, who often feel sidelined as spectators while the P5 fail to find common ground to address these particularly complex situations.

Arguably, the Council incurs in dereliction of its duties as the major players seem to privilege their national foreign and domestic policy agendas (in the case of the Western countries, often shaped by domestic public opinion and the media) or simply their more narrowly defined interests over the common duty of maintaining the international order. In fact, Article 24(2) of the Charter is clear in obligating members of the Security Council to act "in accordance with the Purposes and Principles of the United Nations." But these guidelines are not very precise, since member states will invariably argue that their national policy objectives are grounded in the same ideals as those underlying the purposes and principles of the Charter. Be that as it may, the differing policy agendas make it difficult to reach agreements in addressing certain issues before the Security Council, to the profound frustration of many of the United Nations' member states, and signaling to the international community at large the increasing irrelevance of the Council in maintaining international peace and security.

To add insult to injury, the Council, or rather its member states, are not held accountable to the international community they are meant to serve.[37] Rather, as mentioned in Chapter 7, much of the accountability is geared to the domestic constituency of each member state, whose demands to their respective governments in favor of certain actions may or may not be compatible with the aims of the common membership of the United Nations. This is the central tension that the Security Council faces, which often translates into effective or, to the contrary, ineffective outcomes. It appears that since 2014, the tendency has been moving in the direction of the latter, given the growing list of conflicts which the Council has not been able or willing to address.

Other aspects of the system of governance

What becomes increasingly clear to incoming elected members is that the system of governance of the Security Council is radically different than what they had experienced in the other intergovernmental bodies of the United Nations. The two-tier system in the decision making can translate into either a detonator for "prompt and effective action"[38] (in cases of agreement between the P5) or an intractable obstacle (in case of serious disagreement, especially between some of the P5). The limited size of 15 members is, of course, an added boon to agility. In addition, the high stakes involved in decision-making, when often life and death situations hang in the balance, constitute a powerful incentive for a business-like atmosphere and the adoption of action-oriented resolutions, presidential statements, press statements, or *communiqués*. Often these texts are negotiated within 24 hours or less through well-established procedures, whereby the political coordinators of member states act as rapid clearing-houses of the consultations. When the political coordinators or their experts fail to reach agreement, the question rapidly gets kicked upwards, either to deputy permanent representatives or to the permanent representatives. By normal UN standards, decision-making at the Security Council is swift and efficient. Nonetheless, in the case of resolutions and presidential statements, careful readers will often find perhaps an excess of rhetorical invocations in contrast to practical actions to address the matters at hand.

Indeed, in spite of the business-like atmosphere described above, there still is room in the Security Council for some of the ritual, theatrics, and posturing observed in the other principal intergovernmental organs, as delegations put forth their positions on any given subject in prepared statements, not only in the formal gathering but sometimes even in the informal meetings held out of view of public scrutiny. The author found that there is less serious inter-active discussion in these informal meetings than one would expect on such important matters. In part, this might be explained by an environment of reluctant acceptance on the part of most elected members that, while they can influence the final outcome in specific language, they cannot realistically stop a common position of the P5, unless seven elected members band together to vote against it (the only "veto" the E10 dispose of, but up to now never explicitly used).

Another factor at play is the extremely heavy and unrelenting work load that delegations face, which engenders a certain anxiety to move on quickly. The ritualistic component is even more markedly on display in the debates open to the full membership, which often becomes quite tedious in spite of fulfilling an important function of exposing the Council to a greater diversity of opinions on any given topic. The tediousness is only partially mitigated by the practice of limiting interventions to 4 minutes or less.

Organizational questions

Much of the work of the Security Council is guided by the "Provisional Rules of Procedure" (they have remained "provisional" since their adoption in 1946) and by the practices and agreed measures that make up the working methods, which are periodically updated.[39] As mentioned before, the Council has a relatively large group of subsidiary bodies. At last count, there were 18 sanctions committees,[40] the Counter-Terrorism Committee, the Non-Proliferation Committee, the Military Staff Committee, and various other commissions and working groups as well as the International Criminal Tribunal for the former Yugoslavia (ICTY) and the International Criminal Tribunal for Rwanda (ICTR) (both in their final phases at the time of writing). In addition, there are standing committees and *ad hoc* bodies. All of these bodies report at least once a year—some more frequently—to the Security Council, which tends to either take note of same or act on the specific actions they propose. The P5 collectively decide on the distribution of the chairmanship of these bodies, mostly among the elected members.

The Security Council is often criticized for its inability to adapt to changing circumstances, but the author found that this criticism is somewhat exaggerated, especially in the sphere of updating policies.

For example, there have been highly significant innovations in the manner in which peace operations are run since the report of the Panel on United Nations Peace Operations (the "Brahimi Report") was issued in the year 2000,[41] notably including the increasing importance dedicated to the protection of civilians.[42] The Council has also incorporated numerous thematic themes into its agenda—rule of law, protection of civilians, women in conflict, children in conflict, sexual violence in conflict—as well as dealing with emerging threats such as piracy, organized crime, the potential consequences of climate change, and, of course, terrorism. Thus, new frontiers in dealing with conflict-prone situations and threats to international peace and security have been opened.

Further, and as indicated below, there has also been an evolution in how the Council organizes its work and distributes it among its members, as well as expanding its engagement with non-members and civil society through the Arria-formula consultations.[43] In short, contrary to perceptions from the outside, the Council does show considerable ability to adapt to changing circumstances, in spite of its rigid system of membership.

On the matter of transparency

Much is made of the lack of transparency in the work of the Security Council, in terms of its relatively secretive ways, real or perceived. Over time, different countries and groupings of countries have come forth to lobby in favor of greater transparency. For example, in May 2013, a cross-regional group made up at that time of 22 member states launched what they called the Accountability, Coherence, and Transparency Group (ACT), which focused its efforts on improving working methods and demanding greater accountability. This is one of the areas where the author had sympathized with those demanding greater transparency but, upon joining the Council, found that things were actually moving in the right direction. The progress achieved in recent years may be due, in part, to the permanent members of the Council actually addressing the demands of greater transparency in many different ways (more frequent open debates, more informal interactive dialogues, more regular explanations on the part of the rotating presidencies to member states and the media on what was going on), and even in bigger part to rapidly improving access to information.

The fact was that much progress has been achieved in "opening up" the work of the Council to the perusal of other member states of the United Nations, academia, and civil society at large. Five important elements add up to this relatively greater transparency. First, the continuing evolution of the Council's working methods, last updated in 2010.[44] Second, a greatly improved web-site of the Security Council, with abundant information, including records of all formal meetings, the text of the reports of the Secretary-General addressed to the Council, the Council's formal outputs, and general data.[45] Third, the appearances of an outside publication, the Security Council Report, established in 2004, which has done an admirable job in complying with its mission statement of "making available timely, balanced, high quality information about the activities of the Council and its subsidiary bodies; by convening stakeholders to deepen the analysis of issues before the Council and its working methods and performance ..."[46] Fourth, in recent years a culture of information has sprouted among many elected members, who feel obligated to brief other like-minded countries without divulging restricted information. For example, the delegation of Guatemala briefed the Latin American and Caribbean Group members on a regular basis. Finally, the practice of open sessions has continued to expand, perhaps too rapidly as far as the P5 members are concerned.

In addition to all of the above, it has become increasingly difficult to prevent "leaks" of what is going on in the Council chambers as the use of social media networks has become so ubiquitous. In summary, if the Council was perceived as some type of secret cult a few decades ago, at present any member of the UN community has numerous windows to keep abreast of its work with a certain degree of detail.

Relations with other principal organs

While the Security Council is only one of the principal organs of the United Nations, in practice it functions with great independence. There is a formal provision in Articles 15 (1) and 24 (3) of the Charter mandating that the Security Council present a yearly report to the General Assembly on its activities, which the latter "shall receive and consider." These verbs—"receive" and "consider"—hardly establish any type of supervisory role or even imply a level of accountability on the part of the Security Council to the General Assembly. In fact, the yearly reports of the Security Council have been reduced to a mere formality, with factual information, minimal analysis, and no hint of accountability.

The wider membership is very much aware of this fact, and bemoans it in the statements that numerous delegations present when the report is submitted under agenda item 30, usually in the second or third week of November of each year.[47] In fact, on at least one occasion, one of the author's colleagues on the Security Council in 2012, Peter Wittig, the permanent representative of Germany, decided to innovate, taking advantage of the fact that Germany held the presidency of the Council in September, the month the report had to be finalized in order to be submitted to the consideration of the General Assembly. He envisaged a more analytical report and, in consequence, a more substantial debate in the General Assembly, trying to "move the goal post somewhat in the direction of an element of accountability of the Security Council to the General Assembly."[48] Predictably, this effort had little impact, even in 2012, and even less in subsequent years. Other areas where the Security Council and the General Assembly do interact, as already mentioned, are in matters related to troop contributions and even more importantly in those related to the budget. These two areas of interaction are, indeed, significant, especially in the budgetary implications derived from Security Council resolutions. But it is to be noted that the delegations of P5 countries in the fifth committee of the General Assembly exercise their full leverage to make sure that peace operations are properly funded.

The links between the Security Council and the Economic and Social Council are even more tenuous. As mentioned in Chapter 5, Article 65 of the Charter limits ECOSOC's role to furnishing information or assisting the Security Council "upon its request." As noted, such requests have been few and far between. In the same vein, the important role that the Charter assigned to the Security Council in Article 83 in its relation with the Trusteeship Council is no longer relevant.[49] There are some significant links between the Security Council and the International Court of Justice, which is one of the principal organs of the United Nations, and clearly offers one path towards the peaceful resolution of conflicts and even preventing conflicts.[50] In addition, the link is one of the very few instances in which the General Assembly and the Security Council appear to be on even playing fields on two matters: the intricate process of electing the Judges set up in the Statute of the International Court of Justice—Article 8 of the Statute indicates that "The General Assembly and the Security Council shall proceed independently of one another to elect the members of the Court"[51]—as well as in the capacity of both organs to request advisory opinions—an initiative that the Charter bestows on them in Article 96.

On the other hand, the engagement between the secretariat and the Security Council is frequent, diversified, and rather complex. Clearly, it is the intergovernmental organ that is in charge, with the secretariat carrying out its mandates and monitoring results, as well as reporting back to the Council. However, the secretariat counts with the explicit capacity to take initiatives, under Article 99 of the Charter.[52] In practice, at least in 2012–2013, the secretariat appeared to be kept on a fairly short leash, although the inherent tension between the Council and the secretariat around the issue of delegation of authority varied greatly, from situation to situation, and also over time.

This is not the place to analyze in detail the cause-and-effect relationship between the intergovernmental organ and the secretariat, given the complexity of the matter. However, the author draws one conclusion from his observation of the dynamics at work during 2012–2013, in that when the secretariat's initiatives hold promise for success the Council appears to willingly support them, and when the contrary is the case, the initiatives found little support on the part of the Council. Of the numerous examples that could be cited, only two are offered. The first is the relatively successful initiatives undertaken by the Secretary-General in addressing the growing political and humanitarian crisis that was taking place in the Eastern part of the Democratic Republic of Congo towards the end of 2012, especially in North and South Kivu. This was due to the incursion of rebels,[53] which gave rise to a large number of displaced persons and allegations of involvement of the Governments of Rwanda and Uganda. The Secretary-General dispatched his *Chef de Cabinet*, Susana Malcorra, to the region, and she was successful in partnering with the International Conference on the Great Lakes Region (ICGLR), in brokering an agreement that eventually became the Peace, Security, and Cooperation Framework, which was signed in Addis Ababa on 24 February 2013 by 11 heads of state or their representatives.[54] On 18 March, the Secretary-General announced the appointment of Mary Robinson as his special envoy for the Great Lakes Region, and on 28 March 2013 the Security Council supported the Cooperation Framework through adopting resolution 2098 (2013).

On the other hand, in more or less the same period—October of 2012—the Secretary-General decided to designate Romano Prodi as his Special Envoy for the Sahel region as a way of "shaping and mobilizing an effective United Nations and international response to the complex crisis plaguing the countries and people of this region."[55] Some governments were perplexed by this appointment, since there were other regional and national presences of the United Nations in the sub-region. Although a United Nations Integrated Regional Strategy for the region was eventually produced, the initiative never found much traction on the part of the Council, and by the end of 2013 Mr. Prodi withdrew from his post, and the activities assigned to him were subsequently absorbed by the United Nations Office for West Africa (UNOWA).

As for the Secretary-General himself, he engaged frequently with the Council, offering briefings at formal sessions. He also participated in a monthly luncheon with all members, as well as a yearly retreat of a day and a half. He met with members of the Council, especially the permanent members, individually or collectively. There were also numerous occasions in which the inherent tensions between the Secretary-General and one or more members of the P5 were put on display, confirming Kofi Annan's oft-repeated wistful comment that the P5 perceived him more as a "secretary" than as a "general." On the other hand, most of the elected members, including the author, would have preferred a larger diplomatic role for the Secretary-General, and often pushed in that direction: one more cleavage between the P5 and the E10, although with somewhat blurred frontiers.[56]

Other senior officials of the secretariat interacted even more frequently with the Council, both in formal and informal consultations. Among these the most regular interlocutors seemed to be the heads of the departments of political affairs, of peacekeeping operations, of field support, and of the Office for Coordination of Humanitarian Affairs (OCHA), as well as the High Commissioners for Human Rights and for Refugees. Frequent briefings were also received from Special Representatives of the Secretary-General (SRSG) in the field.

Another crucial function of the secretariat is to prepare the reports which form the basis of the Council's deliberations; yet one more expression of its selective capacity to take initiatives. Most of these reports are available to all member states of the United Nation. The author found significant disparities in their quality and usefulness, which ranged from excellent to substandard.

In summary, in the always fascinating engagement between the secretariat and the intergovernmental organs at the United Nations, the Security Council offered a privileged arena to witness and track the intricate and changing interactions between delegates—on an individual or collective basis—and representatives of the secretariat.

On the legitimacy of the Security Council

It is somewhat surprising that such a maligned institution as the Security Council continues to conserve its legitimacy to a large degree, at least if the criterion is the willingness of the broader membership to abide by the Council's decisions. This organ has been widely accused of being undemocratic, anachronistic, unaccountable to anyone, often ineffective, increasingly irrelevant, and not acting in representation of the wider membership, since the national priorities of the permanent members seem to override the collective responsibilities of the Council to maintain international peace and security.[57] Indeed, the clash of national priorities/interests of some of the permanent members with their collective responsibility, a matter addressed above, is perceived as a real obstacle for the Council to meet its Charter obligations. The more severe critics of the Council have been predicting for some time that its collapse is imminent, given the increasing weight of its inability to act is some of the most notorious threats to peace, such as those that have erupted in the past few years in the Middle East, the Horn of Africa, the Korean Peninsula, and other parts of the globe.

And still, in spite of all its obvious flaws, the Council keeps functioning on a regular and sometimes even frenetic basis. Its decisions adopted under Chapter VII are observed by the vast majority of member states and even by individuals targeted by sanctions.[58] As was already noted, nine out of every ten resolutions are adopted by unanimity. But more importantly, the Council has contributed successfully to impede conflagrations of a global scale for the past 70 years.

As far as the author could perceive from his perch in the Council, its only source of real legitimacy is the Charter itself. In other words, member states do not necessarily respect the Security Council, but they apparently do respect the United Nations Charter that created it. They do so in full recognition of two facts. First, the international environment today is not ready to significantly amend the Charter, and much less to adopt a new one. In consequence, and, second, the Charter and its principal organs, including the Security Council, are perceived as "the only game in town." Expressed differently, there is acute awareness that in the absence of the Charter and its institutions, a breakdown in the existing world order would become an even greater risk. That is why the Security Council, warts and all, is tolerated as a flawed arrangement, while hopes of its eventual reform never wane.

Security Council reform

The above brings up one of the most divisive and long-running debates going on in the United Nations: Security Council reform. This is another area where the author held fairly firm views on the matter, but where being exposed to the work of the Council gave him some pause in continuing to espouse those views. The following paragraphs are not so much about Security Council reform, but try to explain why the author is cautiously re-visiting previously held convictions.

As is well know, Security Council reform has been on the agenda of the General Assembly since 1993. The background is built on the original discontent with the extreme asymmetries between permanent and elected members, including the problematic aspect of the veto. Frustrations grew over time, as the Council increasingly reflected a bygone era in contrast to the twenty-first century, where the vanquished in the Second World War had become major players in their own right, and new emerging powers had equally become significant global actors. Further, since the 1960s, many new nations had become members of the United Nations, leading to questions of under-representation of some regions and over-representation of others on the Council. In addition, with the end of the Cold War the Council had acquired a new significance; although the nature of conflicts was changing, the role of the Council was taken much more seriously and edging it closer to its original intention (albeit in a totally different context) as conceived in the Charter. Finally, with the expansion of membership in the United Nations at large, from 51 in 1945 to 113 in 1963 (the year that membership in the Security Council was expanded from 11 to 15)[59] to 193 at present, there was growing awareness that 15 members of the Security Council was a very reduced number to "act on the behalf" of an expanded General Assembly.

However, as is also well known, conflicting interests of different players have ended up paralyzing action on this matter, and after over 20 years of consultations and negotiations in different settings, member states are no closer to reforming the Council than they were in 1993. There are essentially six broad categories of positions, with some overlapping. The first is made up of existing permanent members, who understandably are reluctant to give up their privileges and are even more reluctant to share them with newcomers.[60] The second category focuses on expansion in the number of both permanent and elected members; this group of countries is spearheaded by Brazil, Germany, India, and Japan (the G4). The African Group, with its 54 member states, has a special take on this matter, demanding a larger level of representation in both permanent and elected members. A third category takes the opposite position: its members promote expansion, but only of elected members. Originally led, among others, by Italy, Argentina, Canada, Egypt, Mexico, and Pakistan, it has now evolved into the "United for Consensus Group." A fourth category is the so-called G69. It derives its name from the draft document number "L.69" that 22 developing countries from Asia, Africa, and Latin America tabled in 2007–2008, which led to the initiation of the Intergovernmental Negotiation (IGN) process (still ongoing in 2016). Since then, the group has more than doubled in number. The group is focused on achieving lasting and comprehensive reforms of the UN Security Council, and in coordinating the positions of its members in the framework of the IGN process. However, it is also committed to the expansion in both the permanent and non-permanent categories of membership of the Security Council, so there is some overlapping with the G4. In fact, India has played a leadership role in the G69. A fifth category of undeterminable size, also overlapping with other categories, is made up of countries "sitting on the fence" somewhere between the G4 and UFC. These countries could live with either arrangement, although some lean in the direction of the G4 while others lean in the direction of the UFC. And, finally, a sixth group of countries, not mutually exclusive of the previous categories, places the emphasis on transparency, asking for reforms in working methods and procedures. For example, what in 2012–2013 was called the S-5 (Costa Rica, Jordan, Lichtenstein, Singapore, and Switzerland) had consistently promoted more transparency and coordination between the Security Council and the General Assembly. This effort has been continued by the Accountability, Coherence, and Transparency Group mentioned above.

The author's positions on Security Council reform kept evolving over time, but could be considered mainstream for numerous countries that do not have a direct stake in the matter. Like most of his colleagues, he found the veto reprehensible, although he understood that it was unrealistic to expect its elimination, or even some minor concessions that would limit its application.[61] He accepted the idea of an expansion in the membership, but believed that it should be a modest expansion, in the interest of agility. He started out as a firm believer in expanding only the elected members category, but ended up accepting the possibility of expansion in both categories, although he doubted that this was a realistic alternative. And he naturally supported the calls for greater transparency and, even more importantly, greater accountability on the part of the Council's members both for their actions and their inactions (the Rwandan and Srebrenica genocides in 1994–1995 being the most notorious examples of the latter).

As stated, participating in the Council's work gave the author some pause in his conviction of previously held positions, based on his observations. None of his insights imply a radical departure, but rather more nuanced positions. The following reflections are offered more in the mode of "food for thought" than in specific proposals. The reflections revolve around the main categories that shape the debate.

On the veto, the only insight received was the vivid confirmation that for the existing permanent members, and especially the United States and the Russian Federation, the existence of Article 27 (3) (as well as Article 108) is a *sine qua non* condition for their participation in the United Nations. Neither can contemplate subordinating its national interests to a binding decision of an international organization made up of member states, and the oft quoted statement of Secretary of State Cordell Hull in 1944 during hearings in the US Congress continues to ring true today, when he declared that "our Government would not remain there a day without retaining its veto power."[62]

But perhaps more importantly, all five permanent members perceive the veto as the indispensable condition to commit them to the principle of acting on behalf of collective security, knowing full well that in an imperfect world such a principle can be limited by arbitrary behavior on the part of any permanent member, induced by national interests. In other words, the veto can be construed as a necessary evil to avoid something even worse: for one or more of the major players to walk away from the United Nations and engage in unilateral actions. This does not mean approval of the veto, but is more an expression of realism in accepting, reluctantly, that the veto power of the existing P5 is here to stay for understandable reasons, as seen from the P5 perspective, and even defensible reasons, as seen from the rest of the membership's perspective, given the alternatives.

This, in turn, raises the question whether the veto should be extended to other countries that aspire to permanent status, including the same privileges as those accorded to the existing P5, a matter linked to the second big issue on the Security Council reform agenda: whether expansion of membership should occur in both categories or only in the category of elected members. The author had difficulty reconciling his grudging acceptance of the expansion of permanent members with the privilege of the veto power, while at the same time finding the veto power objectionable in the first place. He came to believe that extending veto powers to new permanent members could magnify the problem, tying-up the decision-making process even more, by diversifying the number of countries that for any reason, justifiable in their eyes or not, could lead to serious gridlock.

Some of the countries that aspire to permanent status could, of course, drop the insistence of the veto power in a spirit of compromise, although that by itself would lead to a new category of membership (i.e., permanent members with veto power, permanent members without veto power, and elected members). And the acceptance of three categories, it could be argued, starts nibbling away at the edifice of expansion in both categories. Less questionable is the idea of expanding the Council in the category of elected members, and here an important innovation—already proposed in the course of the negotiations on reform and by numerous academics[63]—could consist of creating what has been dubbed an "intermediate category" of major players that could have longer tenures and even stand for re-election. The "intermediate category" comes in various guises and proposals, but their essence is to open a third category, distinct from the present P5 and E10. This intermediate category would meet part of the demands of the countries that now aspire to permanent status, but falls far short of their aspiration to the identical privileges of the existing P5. Still, these countries would have to ask themselves whether such a solution is not preferable to the current stalemate, which could take many years to play out. The author, for one, who had steadfastly rejected the idea of any type of "intermediate" solution when joining the Council, had come around to the idea that it would not be such a bad outcome after all. It would, however, require major concessions on the part of those countries that seek the identical standing as the existing five permanent members, which also appears an unlikely prospect in the coming years.

Another argument frequently put forth is that in its division between permanent and elected members, the Security Council reflects the world of 1945, and not the present. And it is true that many countries have emerged as major players on the world stage, especially if their size, influence, and economic weight are taken into account as suitable metrics. However, if the main criterion used to acquire permanent status in the Security Council is military might, it turns out that today's world does not look all that different than 1945: the United States and the Russian Federation, plus an ascendant People's Republic of China, are still the undisputable major players. If the principal criterion to be a permanent member is military capacity instead of geographical representation, it would be India that has the strongest claim for permanent membership; if geographical balance is brought into the mix, it would be France and the United Kingdom that might be hard pressed to justify their present status, given the over-representation of the Western European countries on the Council.

On the matter of the size of the Council, arriving at a responsible figure for expansion requires balancing the merits of a small and agile organ with the merits of a more diverse and representative organ. Intuitively, that would mean increasing the number of elected members by at least five and no more than ten members, with a distribution of the original P5, an additional five elected for longer periods with the possibility of re-election, and anywhere from 10 to 15 elected members for two-year terms (or longer). The number of variations on these themes is infinite, and they can only be resolved by direct negotiations. As noted earlier, this discussion also feeds into the controversial matter of some regions being "over-represented" and others "under-represented."

In short, the author left the Security Council with ambiguous feelings regarding the question of reform. On the one hand, he continued to be pessimistic about the viability of change, given the intense polarization of views on the matter, which tend to favor the *status quo* as the fallback position. On the other hand, the erosion of the Council's credibility and the growing frustration with the *status quo* may eventually break the logjam and allow for a revisiting of the matter in a more flexible attitude to find consensual solutions.

As to the lack of transparency, the author's concerns were more centered on the lack of accountability. The Council does not appear to be any more accountable today to the broader membership and the international community at large than it was during its founding years. This no doubt is due to the fact that, when national interests are at play over the principle of collective security, the major players feel accountable only to their domestic constituencies, rather than to the international community at large.

On the final matter of improved working methods, the author found that decision-making was still heavily weighted in favor of the interests of the P5, but trending in a favorable direction towards more inclusion. For example, by 2012–2013, the P5 had pulled back considerably in their previous efforts to neutralize the working group on procedure and documentation, which was pushing for the advancement of innovations and best practices. Also, the custom of limiting the capacity of initiative to the permanent members, such as reflected in the figure of the "pen holder," has gradually ceded somewhat to the elected members. During the author's tenure on the Council, both Togo and Australia were "allowed" to become pen holders (on resolutions referring to Guinea-Bissau and Afghanistan, respectively), as was Guatemala on the Informal Working Group on International Tribunals, which dealt with the tribunals of ex-Yugoslavia and Rwanda. The practice of assigning elected members as "pen holders" was expanded during the period 2014–2015. The evolving content of the Working Methods Handbook is another positive example.

Conclusion

There is little doubt that the Security Council is a flawed organ, just as there is little doubt that the United Nations is a flawed organization. Most of the serious challenges the Council faces are a result of decisions incorporated into the Charter, in contrast to other parts of the organization, where many of the challenges can be addressed, and even corrected without amending the Charter. It is also the organ where the tension between the common interests of all members and the national interests of the "major players" is most pronounced. Still, the Security Council continues to play an important role in addressing the ideal of the United Nations itself, which includes "saving succeeding generations from the scourge of war." In that respect, in the absence of the Security Council a breakdown in the existing world order would become an even greater risk. It is probably due to that reason that member states are still eager to join the Council; in some of the regional groupings, countries have announced their candidatures for the early 2030s. Thus, the wider membership has faced the conundrum of "not throwing out the baby with the bath water" syndrome, in tolerating a flawed organ in order to conserve a noble and admirable ideal.

Notes

1 Although of the present 93 member states, over one-third (68 members) have never served on the Council.
2 A brief article which describes some of the salient features of Guatemala's activities in the Security Council during 2012–2013 can be found in: Gert Rosenthal, "La Participación de Guatemala en el Consejo De Seguridad de las Naciones Unidas en 2012–2013", *Revista Política Internacional* (Guatemala: Acadēmia Diplomática, Septiembre, 2016, I), 9–25.
3 To illustrate this remark, see the two monumental publications sponsored by the International Peace Institute: *The UN Security Council: From the Cold War to the 21st Century*, David Malone (editor) (Boulder, Col.: Lynne Rienner, 2004), 649 pages; and the updated version: *The UN Security Council in the 21st Century* Sebastian von Einsiedel et al. (eds) (Boulder, Col.: Lynne Rienner, 2016), 876 pages.
4 See: John Vance Langmore, "Can Elected Members Make a Difference in the UN Security Council? Australia's Experience in 2013–2014" *Global Governance* 22, No. 1 (2016), 59–77; Hardeep Singh Puri, *Perilous Interventions: The Security Council and the Politics of Chaos* (Noidia, India: Harper Collins Publishers: 2016).
5 As noted in the previous chapter, the Latin American and Caribbean Group (GRULAC) is assigned two of the ten elected seats on the Council, one each elected in alternate years.
6 That was the position adopted by Mexico, at least between 1947 and 1979, due to its opposition during the negotiations of the Charter to the designation of permanent members with veto power. The government took the quite deliberate decision not to participate in the Council until 1979, when, as indicated in Chapter 5, a contest between Cuba and Colombia ran to 155 ballots, with the stalemate finally being resolved with the withdrawal of both and the election of Mexico as a compromise candidate. Since then, Mexico has been a member of the Council on three occasions.

7 The Latin American and Caribbean Group was represented at the time by Chile and Mexico. Both governments resisted strong *démarches* at the highest levels of their administrations to support the US position, but after the latter failed to gain the required vote, the Permanent Representatives of both countries were subsequently recalled, given the ill-will that was generated within the Council and the need to repair the damaged bilateral relations.

8 As an anecdotal consequence of this role, Guatemala led the opposition to a *démarche* that came from the African Union and the Government of Kenya asking the Security Council to request the International Criminal Court to defer the investigation and prosecution against President Uhuru Muigai Kenyatta and Deputy President William Samoei Ruto, a prerogative that neither the Charter nor the Rome Statute contemplates. The draft resolution was defeated by a vote of 8 to 7. See: S/PV.7060, 15 November 2013.

9 See: S/PV.6849, 17 October 2012. Also see: *Security Council Report, Cross-Cutting Report* (2013, 1, 18 January 2013) 4–5.

10 See, for example: *Letter dated 13 March 2013 from the Chair of the Informal Working Group on International Tribunals addressed to the President of the Security Council* (S/2013/159) 14 March 2013.

11 Security Council resolutions 827 (1993) and 955 (1994)), respectively.

12 Colin Keating makes the same point, when he says: "it needs to be said that despite the formidable obstacles that have evolved in Council process and in the power dynamics between elected and permanent members, a number of small countries have demonstrated in recent years that it is nevertheless still possible to assert a leadership role. Austria, Costa Rica, Denmark, Guatemala and Uganda are some of several countries that have distinguished themselves in this regard." Colin Keating, "Power Dynamics between Permanent and Elected Members" *The UN Security Council in the 21st Century* (Boulder, Col.: Lynne Rienner Publishers, Inc. 2016) 152.

13 Until 2016, elections were held in the General Assembly in the third week of October, giving newly elected members roughly 8 to 10 weeks to prepare themselves. But on 10 September 2014 the General Assembly adopted resolution 68/307 on the Revitalization of the work of the General Assembly. Among other aspects, it decided to "conduct the elections of the non-permanent members of the Security Council ... about six months before the elected members assume their responsibilities" (op. 17).

14 Guatemalan staff was benefited by extensive briefings from Loraine Sievers, a former (retired) Chief of the Security Council Secretariat Branch.

15 See: *Presidential Note on Working Methods*, S/2010/507, 26 July 2010, paragraph 76. In case an incoming country is scheduled to assume the Presidency in January, it will be invited to sit in on all meetings for eight weeks.

16 The responsibilities are assigned collectively through one of the P5 members in charge of consultations regarding the distribution of subsidiary bodies. This role was played by the US in 2012 and by the UK in 2013.

17 The E10 representatives chairing the sanctions committees largely set the tone and agenda for committee activities. See: Sue Eckert, "The Role of Sanctions," *The UN Security Council in the 21st Century*, (Boulder, Col.: Lynne Rienner, 2016) 413–439.

18 Kishore Mahbubani, "The Permanent and Elected Council Members" in David Malore (ed.) *The UN Security Council: From the Cold War to the 21st Century* (Boulder, Col.: Lynne Rienner Publishers, 2004), 258.

19 Mahbubani, "The Permanent and Elected Council Members," 259.

20 For the full text, see: S/PV.6943, 28 March 2013.

21 Colin Keating, "Power Dynamics between Permanent and Elected Members" especially 146–147. "It was never politically easy in the Security Council in the early 1990s to stand up against the momentum of one or more P5 members seeking an outcome. But neither was it politically impossible. It seems that during the 2000s this equation changed radically for most elected members ... It is clear that the level of control of the Council by the P5 expanded during this period and was matched by an increasing marginalization of the elected members."

22 Resolution 377A (V), 3 November 1950. Part A indicates: "*Resolves* that if the Security Council, because of lack of unanimity of the permanent members, fails to exercise its primary responsibility for the maintenance of international peace and security in any case where there appears to be a threat to the peace, breach of the peace, or act of aggression, the General Assembly shall consider the matter immediately with a view to making appropriate recommendations to Members for collective measures, including in the case of a breach of the peace or act of aggression the use of armed forces when necessary, to maintain or restore international peace and security ..."

23 See: General Assembly resolution 70/262 and Security Council Resolution 2282 (2016), both adopted on 27 April 2016.

24 In 2012, of the 55 resolutions adopted, 48 had unanimous votes and one was adopted by consensus (without putting it to the vote); an additional four were adopted by majority vote. In 2013, of the 48 resolutions adopted, 43 had unanimous votes, and four were adopted by majority vote. One was not adopted. In 2012 two resolutions were vetoed; in 2013 none were.

25 The drafter (pen holder) of a Security Council resolution can take the decision, once the text is available in blue, to disseminate it to the wider membership and to seek cosponsors. The covering letters requesting cosponsors are known as "rule 37 letters".

26 See: S/PV.6484, 18 February 2011. This was the 14th time since 1990 that the United States had vetoed a draft resolution involving the Palestinian-Israeli issue.

27 See: S/PV.6498, 17 March 2011. In his explanation of vote, the Representative of Germany stated: "Decisions on the use of military force are always extremely difficult to take. We have very carefully considered the option of using military force—its implications as well as its limitations. We see great risks."

28 Many observers had expected South Africa to vote abstention, due to the country's deep involvement in the African Union's initiatives to mediate a ceasefire in Libya. On the other hand, those initiatives were reflected in operative paragraph 2 of the resolution, which validates the role of the Peace and Security Council of the African Union in facilitating a dialogue to find a peaceful and sustainable solution to the conflict. In his explanation of vote, Baso Sangqu of South Africa said: "As a matter of principle, we have supported the resolution, with the necessary caveats to preserve the

sovereignty and territorial integrity of Libya and reject any foreign occupation or unilateral military intervention under the pretext of protecting civilians. It is our hope that this resolution will be implemented in full respect for both its letter and spirit. This is consistent with the African Union Peace and Security Council decision to respect the unity and territorial integrity of Libya and its rejection of any foreign military intervention, whatever its form." S/PV.6498, 17 March 2011, 10.

29 For a fascinating account of this episode and the events that led up to it, see: Puri, *Perilous Interventions*, Chapter 3, "Lybia: The Unraveling of a Country," 59–103.

30 The Action Group included the Secretaries-General of the United Nations and the League of Arab States, the Foreign Ministers of China, France, Russia, United Kingdom, United States, Turkey, Iraq (Chair of the Summit of the League of Arab States), Kuwait (Chair of the Council of Foreign Ministers of the League of Arab States), and Qatar (Chair of the Arab Follow-up Committee on Syria of the League of Arab States), and the European Union High Representative for Foreign and Security Policy.

31 Again, for an incisive analysis of the factors at play, see: Puri, *Perilous Interventions*, Chapter 4 "Syria: The Multilayered and Still Unfolding Tragedies," 104–136.

32 Russia and China also cast their first veto on the situation in Syria by voting against draft resolution S/2011/612, which the other 13 members of the Council supported. See: S/PV.6627, 4 October 2011.

33 S/PV.6711, 4 February 2012.

34 S/PV.6810, 19 July 2012. Russia and China again vetoed a draft resolution on Syria in May of 2014, this time trying to refer the situation in the Syrian Arab Republic to the Prosecutor of the International Criminal Court. See: S/PV.7180 of 22 May. Draft resolution S/2014/348 received 13 votes in favor and 2 votes against.

35 S/2118 (2013), 27 September 2013.

36 See: S/PV.7138, 15 March 2014. The General Assembly, for its part, adopted a non-binding resolution condemning the annexation: 68/262, 27 March 2014. It was adopted by 100 votes in favor, 11 against and 58 abstentions.

37 An interesting Report, prepared by some 30 Humanitarian and human rights organizations in March of 2016 and titled *Fuelling the fire, How the Security Council's Permanent Members are undermining their own commitments on Syria*, makes the same illustrative point. See: www.oxfam.org/sites/ www.oxfam.org/files/file_attachments/bp-fuelling-the-fire-syria-110316-sum m-en.pdf.

38 As called for by Article 24(1) of the Charter.

39 In 1946 the Council adopted its Provisional Rules of Procedure (S/96). Subsequently these were modified on several occasions; the last revision was made in 1982 (S/96/Rev.7) The working methods are spelled out in notes by the President of the Security Council of 19 July 2006 (S/2006/507), 19 December 2007 (S/2007/749) and 31 December 2008 (S/2008/847), superseded by S/2010/507, 26 July 2010.

40 See: www.un.org/sc/suborg/en/sanctions/information.

41 A/55/305–S/2000/809, 21 August 2000. More recently, a new High-level independent panel on peace operations issued its own review under the title

Uniting our Strengths for Peace: Politics, Partnerships and People, (A/70/95-S/2015/446, 16 June 2015).

42 In this regard, see the *Kigali Principles on the Protection of Civilians,* which emerged from the High-level International Conference on the Protection of Civilians, organized by the Government of Rwanda and held in Kigali on 28–29 May 2015.

43 The "Arria-formula" meetings are informal, confidential gatherings which enable Security Council members to have a frank exchange of views with persons or groups associated with the topics under consultation. See: www.un.org/en/sc/about/methods/arriaformula.shtml.

44 S/2010/507.

45 www.un.org/en/sc/.

46 www.securitycouncilreport.org/. In recent years, the Report has been so complete that it even dispatches a staff member to the periodic trips that the Council makes to visit specific peace operations and sites on the terrain, informing readers on the activities undertaken.

47 See, for example: A/68/PV.56, 21 November 2013, 3.

48 Ambassador Peter Wittig's own words, as narrated to the author on 16 May 2016.

49 "All functions of the United Nations relating to strategic areas including the approval of the terms of the trusteeship agreements ... shall be exercised by the Security Council."

50 In this respect, it should be recalled that the Council receives a yearly briefing from the President of the ICJ.

51 Bruno Simma et al. (ed.), *The Charter of the United Nations* Third Edition (Oxford: Oxford University Press, 2012), 1921–1928, especially paragraphs 58 and 63.

52 The Secretary-General "may bring to the attention of the Council any matter which in his opinion may threaten international peace and security."

53 The rebels were from the *Mouvement du 23 Mars* (M23) and the *Forces armées de la République démocratique du Congo* (FARDC).

54 Angola, Burundi, the Central African Republic, the Congo, the Democratic Republic of the Congo, Rwanda, South Africa, South Sudan, Uganda, the United Republic of Tanzania, and Zambia. In addition, the following four intergovernmental organizations act as guarantors for the Framework: the African Union, the International Conference on the Great Lakes Region, the Southern African Development Community, and the United Nations.

55 Press Release SG/A/1377-AFR/2462-BIO/4423, 10 October 2012.

56 The above remarks deliberately are limited to the period 2012–2013, since the history of the United Nations shows some ebbs and flows in the relationship between the P5 and the Secretary-General, with broad agreement that Dag Hammarskjöld showed the greatest independence, followed by Kofi Annan. See: Simon Chesterman, "Relations with the UN Secretary-General" in *The UN Security Council in the 21st Century*, 443–456.

57 For example, it is often argued that conflicts that do not impinge on the national interests of one or more of the Permanent Members are often ignored. The typical P5 reaction to this argument is that this type of conflict is local, and therefore does not fall within the mandate of maintaining international peace and security.

58 But a few rebel against those decisions, as in the case of the Democratic People's Republic of Korea; or the non-compliance on the part of some states of resolution 1593 (2005), in which the Council decided "that the Government of Sudan and all other parties to the conflict in Darfur, shall cooperate fully with and provide any necessary assistance to the International Criminal Court …" regarding the indictment of Sudanese President Omar al-Bashir.

59 See: General Assembly resolution 1991(XVIII), 17 December 1963.

60 There are some nuances among the five: the United States has signaled in November of 2010 that it could consider granting India permanent status in the Council; the United Kingdom and France seem to be a bit more flexible to exploring options of expansion, while China and the Russian Federation appear quite adamant in resisting expansion.

61 France had begun to promote at the time for P5 members to voluntary abstain from applying the veto in cases which involve mass atrocities; an initiative that has not prospered so far.

62 Edward C. Luck, *Mixed Messages: American Politics and International Organizations, 1919–1999* (Washington, DC: Brookings Institution, 1999), 154.

63 See, for example: Edward Luck, "The Security Council at Seventy: Ever Changing or Never Changing," in *The UN Security Council in the 21st Century* (Boulder, Col.: Lynne Rienner, 2016) 195–214, especially 206–209.

7   An overview

Some lessons learned

- **The essence of multilateral diplomacy**
- **Links between missions and their capitals**
- **Other tools and mechanisms of consensus building**
- **Dealing with asymmetries**
- **The crucial importance of personalities**
- **Dynamics between intergovernmental organs and the secretariat**
- **The question of coherence**
- **The main point of tension (redux)**
- **Conclusion**

This monograph explores the dynamics of decision-making in a multilateral setting. All six chapters seeks to shed some light on how the United Nations functions and how the decisions taken by intergovernmental bodies are translated into deliverable results. As stated in the Introduction, decision-making at the UN is a complex and multifaceted process, since it involves engagement among member states as well as between member states—individually or collectively—and the secretariat. So many factors shape this process that it is difficult to draw specific cause-and-effect relationships that define multilateral diplomacy at the United Nations in a comprehensive and coherent manner. Still, the preceding chapters, which may be taken as case studies, offer some "lessons learned." These cases cover very diverse situations, occurring in different organs and at dissimilar moments in time. Each takes on a singular form of multilateral diplomacy. As was already noted in the Introduction, several cross-cutting systemic factors emerge from the six narratives which are discussed below. In addition, at least four broad characterizations emerge from the text, offering a convenient framework for the subsequent analysis. These are:

1   Despite the legend that has circulated, especially in the 1990s, that the United Nations patrolled the world with unmarked black helicopters to impose its will, the organization, like the vast majority of multilateral institutions—sub-regional, regional, thematic, and global—is unmistakably an intergovernmental body.[1] The United Nations' actions are limited to the collective decisions of its member states (and particularly the most powerful among them); the secretariat, although selectively empowered to take initiatives, is wholly accountable to those collective decisions. Even the actions undertaken by the Security Council that are binding on all members (Article 25) are conceived as collective decisions of the full membership on whose behalf the Council is presumed to act (Article 24 (1)). And the process of building those collective decisions is the main topic of this monograph.

2   It could be said that the organization sits at the apex of all multilateral organizations, given its universal membership, its worthy ideals, and the fact that it generally occupies the moral high ground on global issues. In addition, there is the considerable power vested in one of its intergovernmental organs, the Security Council. More broadly, the United Nations has been a paradigm of multilateralism in almost all areas of human endeavor: economic, social, cultural, environmental, human rights, humanitarian assistance as well as peace and security. In fact, it is in the area of peace and security where the multilateral dimension has a unique significance: first, because commitments on the part of the major powers to multilateralism temper their option to engage in unilateral actions;[2] and, second, because the major powers have to share their multilateral commitments to some degree with other member states, which endows the Council's collective decisions with a stronger dose of legitimacy and at the same time gives smaller countries an opportunity to make a contribution to global stability; an opportunity that many might otherwise not have had.

3   An undeniable strength of the organization is its universality; i.e., virtually all sovereign states on the planet belong to the United Nations. The only condition for membership is for a country to be "peace-loving" and willing to accept the obligations contained in the Charter (Article 4 (1)). However, this strength of the organization is often interpreted as a weakness, especially in Western democratic societies, where frequent criticism is raised at the image of representatives of authoritarian societies playing leadership roles in some of the UN intergovernmental bodies. It is sometimes difficult to explain to casual interlocutors that a truly universal

organization must have room to accommodate all member states, whether or not their systems of governance and values meet or fail to meet certain standards or thresholds. Over the years, it has to be acknowledged that, for better or for worse, to make the United Nations work, universalism and pluralism have had to take precedence over the strict compliance of the lofty standards that the very Charter espouses.

4   A further characterization of the United Nations focuses on the sheer breadth of its aims, which recognizes that saving "succeeding generations from the scourge of war" requires addressing the root causes of armed conflict. The Charter suggests, sometimes explicitly, other times implicitly, that in the long run there can be no peace without development, or without justice, or without respect for human rights, nor can there be development, justice, and respect for human rights without peace. It can be argued that this holistic approach to fulfilling the aims of the Charter is a double-edged sword: both a strength and a weakness of the Organization. It is a strength because it recognizes the linkages between the wide array of human endeavors addressed by the United Nations. It is a weakness because it has overloaded the organization with so many commitments that not only has the gap between expectations and delivery broadened over time, but the continuous quest for greater coherence between the different parts of the organization (as epitomized by "Delivering as one"),[3] added to repeated attempts at reform aimed at attaining the same objective, have by-and-large not yielded the expected results, or at best fallen short of those results. The broadness of the agenda is matched by the geographical reach of the organization, which not only has its central headquarters distributed between New York, Geneva, and Vienna, but also counts with five regional commissions and other organizations located in different parts of the world, as well as a physical presence in around 170 locations.[4]

Some of the more salient factors that the author presents as "lessons learned" are presented below.

The essence of multilateral diplomacy

As is well known, the heart and soul of multilateral diplomacy is networking: among delegates of different member states, between delegates and staff of the secretariat, and between delegates and representatives of academia, civil society, the business sector, and media. In contrast to bilateral diplomacy, where the representatives of any given state engage with government officials and as many representatives of civil society as possible in the place where they happen to be posted, the work of multilateral diplomacy to a large extent takes place among peers, posted, in this particular case, at the United Nations. Almost all member states maintain missions of varying size in New York. All of them, collectively, host the foot soldiers of multilateral diplomacy at the UN and the main actors in the six narratives contained in this monograph.

They are in New York mainly to further the interests and values of their respective countries. In addition, in spite of the considerable differences among them, they join their peers in the collective responsibility of guiding the functioning of the United Nations in the broader common interest of all members as well as the global community at large. Of course, sometimes their national interests and the broader common interests collide, forcing member states to weigh the pros and cons of each alternative goal. This tension is more common to the major players on the world stage, generally in the framework of the Security Council, as illustrated in Chapter 6, but it appears in the daily routine of delegates from all member states, and often contributes to shaping decisions in the General Assembly, and especially in its fifth committee, as illustrated in Chapter 3. But even in the latter case, where the national agenda of a member state prevailed over what most others perceived as the wider common interest, it could be argued— and indeed, the member state whose national interest prevailed did argue—that the long-term stability in budgetary financing assured by the decision was in every member state's interest. This is another way of saying that sometimes the dividing line between the national agendas of individual member states and the collective common interest is not easily definable.

Returning to the "foot soldiers" of multilateral diplomacy, as is well known, the nucleus of national representation of member states revolves around the missions accredited to the United Nations. Each mission is under the responsibility of a permanent representative or his deputy, while the individual duty of each member of the mission is a function of his specific rank and assigned function. In this respect, if the selection process of national diplomats posted in New York is effective, each person would presumably combine professional skills, abilities, and knowledge with the personal attributes to facilitate engagement with his or her peers. Among those personal attributes, the capacity to communicate is crucial. While communication is facilitated during formal sessions through simultaneous interpreters in the six official languages of the United Nations, much of the underpinning of consensus-building occurs in informal settings and even at social gatherings where translation is usually not available (hosting meals and receptions is also part of the toolbox of multilateral diplomacy), so it is important for delegates to be able to work in English, which over the past decades has become the *lingua franca* at the organization.

Since a significant part of the functions of the intergovernmental organs consists in crafting collective decisions, every member state must be prepared to make concessions to accommodate the views of numerous delegations (193, in the case of the General Assembly). In other words, there is no room for dogmatism in multilateral diplomacy, and arriving at collective decisions is at the heart of the matter. It requires time, patience, and even some theatrics, as member states maneuver between realizing their optimum aspirations and their "red line" which would impede their joining a consensus. Perseverance is also important, as illustrated by the ten years that it took for a relatively simple idea of promoting a gathering on financing for development to gain enough traction to coalesce into the Monterrey Conference of 2002 (Chapter 2). The main point is that in spite of its messiness, at the end of the day multilateral diplomacy at the United Nations seems to work most of the time, both at the level of "low politics" and of "high politics" (the latter, mostly in the Security Council). This is one of the "takeaways" of the preceding six narratives.

Links between missions and their capitals

An important aspect of multilateral diplomacy refers to the links between the UN-based missions and their respective ministries. Indeed, a frequent rejoinder of delegates when pressed to take a position during a negotiation is that he or she must consult with "the capital." This only reflects the fact that the delegates in New York do not function as self-contained units, but rather form part of a more-or-less sophisticated organization at the national level that generates what is conventionally called "foreign policy." Of course, the level of control that a ministry of foreign affairs—itself part of a wider system of governance—exerts on its outposts abroad varies significantly from country to country, and also from issue to issue. The higher the profile of the issue and its potential to impact on domestic public opinion, the more control "the capital" will wish to exert. In that respect, for many smaller member states the degree of delegation of authority to their missions in New York is higher than would be the case for larger and more advanced countries, which understandably expect to be consulted on all aspects, large or small, before commitments are undertaken in New York.

The degree of centralization or decentralization of foreign ministries in the adoption of national positions strays far from the topic of this monograph, and it is only mentioned here as part of the intricate process of decision-making at the United Nations. Its relevance to multilateral diplomacy is twofold. First and most obvious, multilateral diplomacy is not limited to the actors posted in New York, since it involves the senior officials of the governments that they represent. This is an area, then, where multilateral diplomacy and bilateral diplomacy intersect. Second, and especially from the smaller country perspective, there is a dilemma, in that the natural inclination of ministries of foreign affairs towards relying more on the advice of their respective mission posted in New York is often countered, especially in higher profile situations, by *démarches* undertaken, usually by one or more P5 member, invoking the bilateral relationship to try to persuade the corresponding member state at the level of its respective capital to support any given position adopted in the multilateral setting. This is a potential arena, then, of differences in perspective between "capitals" and "missions," or, stated differently, a potential source of tensions between bilateral and multilateral diplomacy of member states.

Other tools and mechanisms of consensus building

A topic that is not explicitly touched upon in the preceding chapters but was present in virtually all the cases discussed refers to the considerable efforts that are expended in consensus-building through the use of work-shops, seminars, retreats, and training. These have been powerful instruments to facilitate decision-making at the United Nations. They bring together selected delegates, from the most senior level to the level of experts, to explore issues, confront different points of view, and discuss approximations in what could eventually be a consensus-building exercise, or simply share information and ideas.

Some of these activities take place "in-house" (for example, the courses and seminars offered by the United Nations Institute for Training and Research (UNITAR)), or events sponsored by one or more missions. Others are organized by foundations, non-governmental institutions, and not-for-profit think tanks such as the International Peace Institute, the United Nations Foundation, the Stanley Foundation, the Dag Hammarskjöld Foundation, the Friedrich Ebert Foundation, the Quaker UN Office, and various graduate centers of Universities. Some of the events are brief—an extended luncheon, or one-day work-shops—while others are longer retreats (a favorite location for such events is the Greentree Estate in Long Island). The most substantive (and generous) activity the author participated in on several occasions was the yearly four to five day event organized between 1997 and 2008 by the Stanley Foundation under the banner "Conference on the United Nations of the Next Decade."[5] Not only were these events stimulating, but they developed a spirit of camaraderie among the participants, thus contributing to the subsequent networking they were all engaged in at the United Nations. The use of all of these types of events was present in each of the narratives of this monograph (except, of course, for the one contained in Chapter 5, on electoral politics at the United Nations).

Dealing with asymmetries

In both Chapters 3 and 6, reference is made to George Orwell's celebrated phrase from *Animal Farm*, that "some animals are more equal than others." Indeed, all six narratives contain evidence of the asymmetric nature of interaction at the intergovernmental level, in spite of the principle of "sovereign equality" espoused in Article 2 (1) of the Charter. In part to mitigate the asymmetries, countries have shown a strong propensity to band together in formal and informal groups with a variety of different purposes and memberships. Some of those groupings are based on geographical commonalities,[6] others along common or like-minded interests and still others represent countries in special situations (landlocked, least developed, small island developing states). All are designed to improve the leverage of the individual members in advancing their common agendas at the United Nations. Special mention should be made of the practice of more advanced projects of integration, notably the European Union, but also the Caribbean Community and the African Union, whose members tend to take common positions and often intervene in debates through a single spokesperson.

Although the North-South divide between member states was not quite as pronounced during the years covered in preceding chapters as it was during the last four decades of the twentieth century, the majority of groupings still gather countries that feel at a disadvantage in the decision-making process due to what they perceive as reduced leverage in both economic and political affairs at the global level. Perhaps the most relevant is the Group of 77 and China (G77), a loose coalition of 131 developing countries, designed to promote its members' collective economic interests and create an enhanced joint negotiating capacity in the United Nations. A similar coalition designed to promote its members' collective political interests is the Non Aligned Movement, which represent an even looser coalition of 120 members.

In spite of the heterogeneous nature of membership and the numerous differences that characterize its different constituents, the G77 has managed to play a significant role (but rarely a decisive one) in bridging the North-South divide and mitigating the asymmetries among the full membership of the United Nations. The simple strategy is to intervene in debates—and, often in negotiations—in representation of all members. The rotating presidency of the Group consults the broader G77 membership on a regular basis, especially on higher-profile issues. Quite often, when agreement on any particular position does not receive ample support, the spokesperson of the group desists from intervening in debates or negotiations. In this case, G77 members intervene individually to explain and promote their national positions.[7] A similar arrangement is applied to a limited set of political issues, when the even more heterogeneous membership of the Non Alighted Movement can agree to deliver statements in representation of all members.

While the G77 and even more so the NAM have very diverse positions within their membership on the many issues being considered in the intergovernmental organs of the United Nations, their presence has had both symbolic and real value in the process of consensus-building. Sometimes both G77 and NAM act together under the umbrella of the so-called Joint Coordinating Committee (JCC) established since 1994. Examples of delegations grouping together are illustrated in almost all the narratives contained in this monograph, with perhaps the exception of Chapter 6, since interaction in the Security Council leaves little room for group representations.[8] A particularly successful instance of a grouping acting in representation of its member states is described in Chapter 3, whereby the so-called Río Group (which has since evolved into the Community of Latin American and Caribbean States (CELAC)) played an outsized role in contributing to a consensus on a particularly difficult negotiation. On the other hand, while the 15 members of the Security Council collectively act on behalf of the wider membership of the United Nations, each of those 15 members is guided exclusively by its national position on the issues at hand.

Finally, one of the cross-cutting arguments made in this monograph is that the size of a member state is not necessarily a definer of its capacity to exert influence on the outcome of events. Even very small states such as Barbados, Fiji, and Timor-Leste have shown considerable presence in inter-governmental organs, based not on their size but on the respect that their performance has earned them among their peers. This has also been the experience in the context of the Security Council, where it has been shown that small countries, if well organized, can indeed contribute in a significant manner to that body's work (Chapter 6).

In summary, the narratives contained in this monograph illustrate that there is value to the large amount of groups among developing and developed countries, not only to reach agreements on substantive matters, but to help mitigate the considerable asymmetries that exist among UN member states.

The crucial importance of personalities

If there is one lesson to be learned from the foregoing six narratives, it is found in the crucial importance that personalities play in multilateral diplomacy. It was the personalities involved, more than the rules of procedure or the different formats in which delegates interact, that made the difference in each instance. Examples abound; they include Theo-Ben Gurirab, President of the General Assembly who so forcefully led the 54th session, or Richard Holbrooke of the United States who was the driving force behind the revision of the scales of assessments of the United Nations' budgets, or the crucial role of Mauricio Escanero (Mexico) as the facilitator of the Monterrey Declaration, plus so many other names that populate the preceding pages, including Secretary-General Kofi Annan. Having the right personalities in place, in the intergovernmental organs or in the secretariat, is one of the many random factors that determine whether a specific initiative taken by any government or the secretariat will ultimately succeed.

More broadly, and precisely because multilateral diplomacy is all about networking, what can never be lost from sight is that the "foot soldiers" mentioned above are not only delegates of their respective countries, but they are human beings engaging with their peers and colleagues in pursuit of common goals. Although the leverage they bring with them as a function of the country they happen to be representing varies greatly, the quality of that engagement can go a long way towards creating a constructive environment which facilitates consensus-building and decision-making. This obvious but sometimes overlooked fact is amply illustrated in the six preceding narratives through numerous examples.

Dynamics between intergovernmental organs and the secretariat

One of the most crucial pillars of multilateral diplomacy is the manner in which the intergovernmental organs and the secretariat interact. As stated in the Introduction, the notion that the member states are the collective decision-makers while the secretariat executes the mandates, monitors results, and reports back to the governments is somewhat abstract. The interaction is continuous and at multiple levels:

governments instruct the secretariat to undertake certain actions and the secretariat complies; the secretariat proposes actions and the governments react to the proposals. There are numerous lines of communication taking place simultaneously. Although nominally "the secretariat" is embodied by the Secretary General, in practice delegates interact with numerous representatives of the secretariat on a daily basis. These representatives are made up of cadres of international civil servants. They may be senior officials or the staff that many experts of missions work with regularly. By engaging constructively, these individuals representing member states or those that consider themselves international civil servants stimulate and learn from each other in a kind of dialectic arrangement.

As is well known, some of the work of the secretariat is recurrent (keeping statistics, providing periodic reports, providing logistical support to meetings); another part is in response to specific mandates. Sometimes the engagement between the intergovernmental bodies and the secretariat is fluid and constructive; sometimes it reflects certain tensions when those bodies or some of their individual member states find the performance of the secretariat below expectations, or not sufficiently impartial. The reports prepared by the secretariat are absolutely crucial work instruments, as illustrated repeatedly in the six narratives. Sometimes those reports contain the seminal proposals which help shape decisions, codified in resolutions. Sometimes they contain information regarding the compliance of prior decisions. They are ubiquitous in all intergovernmental bodies and usually accessible not only to delegations but to any interested party on the United Nations' web sites.

There is one specific area of engagement between the intergovernmental bodies and the secretariat that deserves special mention, and that is the engagement between the chairs and their bureaus, on the one hand, and their respective representatives of the secretariat on the other. One of the functions of the latter is to support the enormous amount of meetings, formal and informal, that are held. The secretariat is tasked with organizing the meetings, preparing notes for the chair, and assisting the chair in resolving procedural questions, keeping records of the meetings, and assuring that all the logistical elements are in place. Governments tend to regard these as inherent functions of the secretariat, that fall under the administrative tasks set forth in Article 97 of the Charter. They usually work smoothly, although at times chairs resent what they consider as excessive "coaching" on the part of the representative of the secretariat sitting beside them. Some perceive this as the secretariat trying to encroach on the purview of the Chair.

In addition, the chair-secretariat relationship sometimes spills over into more substantive aspects. For example, the secretariat can propose to the Chair to invite prominent personalities as speakers or briefers to member states on matters of common interest. This tool is frequently used both in the General Assembly and in the Economic and Social Council on matters of general interest—recent events in the global economy, for example—or more focused topics related directly to the agenda item being discussed.

Seen from the angle of member states, although the three principal intergovernmental organs and their numerous subsidiary bodies all function under virtually the same rules of procedure, the exact modalities of engagement may vary somewhat from one body to another and especially so in the case of the Security Council. This holds true in relation to the substantive role the secretariat can play in assisting member states in consensus-building through providing proposals and recommendations, and equally in procedural matters in support of the orderly functioning of the intergovernmental bodies. A key nucleus of interaction occurs at the level of the rotating chair of each body and the assigned member of the secretariat, as illustrated especially in Chapter 4 on the Economic and Social Council.

It should also be noted that the secretariat itself is not a homogeneous block under the clear direction of the Secretary-General. In fact, its departments are numerous and widespread—thematically and geographically—with a rather weak system of coordination from the top. While all the departments, in New York and abroad (including the five regional commissions) are parts of the United Nations secretariat and thus respond hierarchically to the Secretary-General, in practice the representatives of UN intergovernmental bodies and even individual representatives of member states engage continually with numerous representatives of the secretariat. These multiple interactions going on simultaneously can either lead to a coherent outcome where both parts of the organization—the intergovernmental organ and the secretariat—engage smoothly and under common orientations, or they can lead to a more dysfunctional outcome. There are examples of both alternatives in preceding chapters, and the fragmentation they sometimes lead to are mentioned below.

Another crucial element in the quality of the interaction between intergovernmental organs and the secretariat is the degree to which member states are willing to empower the latter by either expanding or limiting its capacity to take initiatives. As stated previously, the Charter describes the Secretary-General as the "chief administrative officer of the organization," and the only capacity of initiative that the Charter bestows on him is limited to "any matter which in his opinion may threaten the maintenance of international peace and security" (Article 99). Further, as mentioned in Chapter 6, at least during 2012–2013 the P5 members preferred to keep the secretariat on a short leash.

In the previous six narratives, the question of engagement between intergovernmental organs and the secretariat comes up repeatedly. As case studies, some very positive outcomes are described, perhaps the most successful one being the Millennium Summit described in Chapter 1, which was the product of a positive interaction between both parts of the organization. The secretariat presented a superior proposal, in the form of *We the peoples: the role of the United Nations in the twenty-first century*. At the same time, the General Assembly was represented, as mentioned above, by a strong interlocutor in the person of its president, and a partnership arrangement was implemented between the intergovernmental organ and the secretariat in codifying the secretariat's proposal into a clear draft proposal which allowed for the adoption of a collective outcome: the Millennium Declaration. The secretariat further built on this declaration by coming up with the proposal—perhaps taking some liberties regarding its capacity to take initiatives—that resulted in the Millennium Development Goals (MDGs), which were subsequently endorsed by the General Assembly.

The case study covered in Chapter 2 which led to the Monterrey Declaration was equally successful in the realm of interaction between the intergovernmental organ and the secretariat, although it was considerably more complex and drawn-out over a two-year period. A closer partnership was built between the secretariat and the Bretton Woods institutions than was the case for the Millennium Summit. In addition, a third important actor appeared in the form of a very proactive host government of the international conference. The intergovernmental representation was somewhat more diffused, with a PGA who delegated part of the function of engagement with the secretariat in the co-chairs of the preparatory committee, and the secretariat itself acting through a designated coordinating office. In contrast, Chapter 3 is a story of the intergovernmental machinery clearly in control, with the secretariat playing a purely supporting role. It is more a narrative on interaction between delegations of member states rather than an interaction between the General Assembly and the secretariat.

Finally, and as stated previously, interaction between the intergovernmental organs and the secretariat is not always smooth or successful. It is in Chapters 4 and 6, which relate the author's perspective of the Economic and Social Council in 2003 and the Security Council in 2012–2013 where some of the systemic issues of coherence come through most forcefully, as explained in the following section.

The question of coherence

A recurrent theme that emerges from the six narratives is the fragmentation that has characterized the work of the United Nations. The author's exposure to all three of the principal intergovernmental organs convinced him that the fragmentation is a systemic failure, which over the lifetime of the organization has been repeatedly addressed with minor and even major initiatives of reform under the banner of "greater coherence, efficiency and effectiveness." Some of those efforts have rendered partial results, but by and large have rarely measured up to expectations.

Paradoxically, this problem finds its origin in the Charter, which clearly separates the intergovernmental decision-making of the three main "pillars" of the United Nations into separate silos. To simplify matters (the reality is more complex, given overlaps in the different organs' remits), the Charter assigns to the Security Council the maintenance of international peace and security; to the Economic and Social Council the promotion and protection of human rights as well as the promotion of development and international economic cooperation; while the General Assembly assumes something akin to the legislative functions of national parliaments in all areas (except those specifically excluded by Article 12), concentrating among other aspects, on setting aspirational global goals, advocating in favor of those goals, setting norms, and simply offering a meeting place for all humanity. There are scarce formal links of coordination and consultation between the three principal intergovernmental organs, but there are some serious areas of overlapping, especially between ECOSOC and the General Assembly.

To make the silo effect even more pronounced, the secretariat's organizational chart mirrors these cleavages, so, again to simplify, the Security Council is supported by the Departments of Political Affairs (DPA), Peacekeeping (DPKO), and Field Support (DFS); while the Economic and Social Council and the General Assembly deal, at least on development matters, with the Department of Economic and Social Affairs (DESA), while the Human Rights Council (since 2006 a subsidiary body of the General Assembly) functions with relative independence in Geneva under the Office of the High Commissioner of Human Rights. The coordination between these Departments is somewhat better than the coordination between the intergovernmental bodies, since they all answer to the Secretary General, and there are some mechanisms of coordination in place, but in practice the departments of the secretariat tend to reinforce the compartmentalization of the principal organs.

The same can be said about the various components of the so-called United Nations Development System, in the areas of technical assistance, humanitarian assistance, advocacy, and norm setting related to development. Most of the programs, funds, and agencies involved in operational activities have their own intergovernmental governance structures, and these, too, lack common strategies and guidance. In fact, tensions between the "development pillar" under the secretariat and the activities of the funds and programs, especially the United Nations Development Programme, enhance and magnify the "silo effect" in which the United Nations operates.[9] The adverse effects of this situation are reflected both at headquarters and in "the field."

Finally, the fragmentation of the United Nations is further reinforced by an intangible factor: the mindset of representatives of member states, who seem to have grown accustomed to the cleavages between the work of the Security Council, the Economic and Social Council, and the General Assembly. During his twelve year transit through the three principal organs of the United Nations, the author experienced discreet changes in his own mindset, from a passive albeit regretful acceptance that it was difficult for these three intergovernmental bodies to work in a coordinated fashion, to a more pro-active stance, believing that member states were at fault—and paying the consequences in substandard performance—for not insisting on greater coherence in the discharging of the United Nations' multiple activities.

It could be argued that matters may have improved somewhat in the past decade, with the transfer of the function of promoting and protecting human rights from ECOSOC to the General Assembly through the transformation of the United Nations Commission on Human Rights into the Human Rights Council.[10] In addition, the General Assembly's decision to create a United Nations Entity for Gender Equality and the Empowerment of Women, under the broader banner of persistent efforts to gain greater system-wide coherence, should also be recalled.[11] This new entity merges the work of four previously distinct parts of the UN system which focused on women in development. Further, and as mentioned in Chapters 3 and 4, there has also been an increased level of joint responsibilities between the General Assembly and ECOSOC to conduct follow-up activities of the Financing for Development process and in servicing the High Level Political Forum, although it is not clear whether this will strengthen the partnership between both organs or end up in the General Assembly simply absorbing some of the most significant activities of ECOSOC, thus contributing to further overlapping. In sum, the quest for greater coherence and coordination continues to this day, without a clear definition of the secular difficulty in deciding "who does what."

The main point of tension (redux)

This overview would be incomplete without repeating one of the main points raised in Chapter 6 regarding a major flaw of the United Nations: the inability or unwillingness of the Security Council to resolve some of the most prolonged and catastrophic conflicts afflicting the world today. As mentioned, while roughly 90 percent of the resolutions of the Council are adopted unanimously, it is the other 10 percent that has included those conflicts—Syria is perhaps the most dramatic example—with their staggering costs in human lives and suffering. The inability or extreme difficulty of the Permanent Members of the Council to reconcile their national and foreign policy agendas with the real or perceived common obligation of maintaining the international order is clearly the major breakdown in multilateral diplomacy at the United Nations. The consequences have not only had incredible costs in real terms, but have impacted adversely on the whole United Nations System, as in this unique area of activity the organization has often proved ineffective in fulfilling its main purposes and principles. Clearly, this situation has impacted adversely on the public perception of the United Nations. As Hardeep Puri notes, when referring to the Security Council's actions on Libya and Syria during 2011–2012: "The UN, an organization that was set up with the intent of saving succeeding generations from the scourge of war ... is today playing the role of a passive bystander as one country breaks international law and another falls prey to unimaginable man-made devastation."[12]

Conclusion

The narratives contained in this monograph describe six different examples of multilateral diplomacy at work in the United Nations. They are meant to shed some light on how decisions are made at the highest level of its intergovernmental organs, and how those decisions are implemented into actions and subsequently monitored. The narratives cover different facets of decision-making in each of the three principal intergovernmental organs (the General Assembly, the Economic and Social Council, and the Security Council), and at different points in time between 2000 and 2014. They all reveal the extreme intricacy of consensus-building which leads to decision-making, given the large number of actors involved, both at the intergovernmental level and at the level of the secretariat, itself a principal organ of the Charter. They also emphasize the important distinctions between the

Security Council and the other two organs in their purview, organization and modalities of decision-making.

The narratives reveal a large, complex and often unwieldy organization, which nevertheless is capable of organizing its work to produce significant results. Consensus-building is often messy and sometimes even dysfunctional, and repeated efforts at introducing greater coherence, efficiency, and effectiveness to the work of the organization have at best fallen short of expectations. There appear to be structural impediments to profound reforms, some of which are illustrated in previous chapters. However, contrary to the perception that the United Nations is incapable of adapting to changing circumstances, the organization has over the years shown willingness and an ability to adapt. This is reflected in the evolving agendas and working methods, in the creation and/or merging of subsidiary bodies, and in the application of specific recommendations that affect policies in different areas, such as peace-keeping, promoting sustainable peace, addressing climate change, the partnering with other multilateral organizations, the UN's advocacy role for different causes, and providing increased access to non-governmental actors to the work of the organization.

At the same time, change tends to come in small, incremental steps rather than in grand and holistic transformations, so there is almost always a lag between evolving concerns and the capacity to address them in a timely manner. This is especially true since the beginning of the present millennium, when the world has had to face astonishingly rapid change—witness the information and communications technologies revolution—with relatively rigid institutions and mindsets to cope with emerging trends.

In balance, the United Nations, like so many other institutions, is one more case of the half-full, half-empty syndrome. Examples of each half appear in every one of the narratives of this monograph. Among the half-full part is the original vision of the United Nations, which appears as relevant today as it was 70 years ago. The very idea encapsulated in the Charter's brief prologue still resonates with today's "we the people." That fact alone leads to a second proposition: the world still needs the United Nations, or, in its absence, something that would take its place. Its tangible contributions to cooperation and stability over its lifetime outweigh its many challenges—the half-empty part—some of which are touched on in preceding pages.

Certainly the above-mentioned inability of the Security Council to come to grips with recent threats to global peace and security fall in that latter category, the most intractable of the challenges portrayed. Many of the other challenges, such as the excessive fragmentation, poor practices in priority setting, and a broken system of budgetary management, can be successfully addressed with sufficient political will on the part of member states and deft management on the part of the secretariat, without necessarily requiring amendments to the Charter.

Thus, the author still views the future of the United Nations with a dosage of guarded optimism. This guarded optimism was further bolstered by the selection of António Guterres of Portugal as the next Secretary-General of the United Nations as this monograph went to press.[13] It is fitting to make a brief closing remark on this matter, since the selection of the chief administrator officer of any multilateral organization, including the United Nations, is both a crucial result of multilateral diplomacy and a potentially powerful indicator of the capacity of the organization to carry out is work in the future.

As is well known, in accordance with article 97 of the Charter, the General Assembly appoints the Secretary-General "upon the recommendation of the Security Council." Historically, this meant that the selection process had to meet the least common denominator that would satisfy the permanent members of the Security Council. For many years, the wider membership of the General Assembly had insisted on greater transparency and accountability in the selection process and during the past two years moved somewhat in that direction by organizing public hearings that gave candidates the opportunity to interact with member states.[14] This, in turn, exerted some pressure on the Security Council to at least take on board the collective reactions of the wider membership to the interventions and responses of all candidates before the General Assembly. In the end, it would appear that the legitimate demands for geographic and gender considerations were subordinated to the principal criteria of selecting the strongest candidate, based on qualifications, temperament, and experience. This is as it should be, since the future direction of the organization depends on it to a large degree. As stated repeatedly throughout this monograph, people do matter; and this fact is singularly true for the "chief administrative officer" of the United Nations.

Notes

1 The European Union, with its hybrid system of supranational and intergovernmental governance, is the main exception.
2 Although not always successfully, as demonstrated in 2003 by the events in Iraq and by the NATO intervention in Kosovo in March of 1999.
3 See, for example: Report of the High-level Panel on United Nations System-wide Coherence in the areas of development, humanitarian

assistance and the environment, *Delivering as One* (A/61/583), 20 November 2006.
4   The author has deliberately avoided bringing the specialized agencies and all the programs into his analysis, since this adds an additional layer of complexity to what is usually referred to as the "UN System." Most of those agencies have their own system of governance and only receive nominal guidance and orientation from the Secretary-General through the Chief Executives Board (CEB), as well as presenting yearly formal reports to ECSOC.
5   The Stanley Foundation continues to be active. See: www.stanleyfoundation.org/.
6   The regional groupings of UN member states to respond to equitable geographical representation in elections do not form part of this discussion, since they normally refrain from engaging in debates on substantive issues.
7   Even when the G77 intervenes through a spokesperson, many individual members feel moved to take the floor to give their own take on any given topic.
8   However, the NAM has a "Caucus" of their members that serve on the Security Council, who meet periodically to "coordinate," but not necessarily to adopt common positions. They also inform the wider membership of NAM on the activities of the Council. In addition, during the open debates of the Council, regional groups, and especially the European Union, may be invited to present collective positions through joint statements.
9   For two interesting analysis of this matter, see: Linklaters, *Governance for the United Nations Developing System: Adapting to meet the challenges of a changing world* (New York, May 2016); as well as the Report of the Independent Team of Advisors (ITA), *ECOSOC Dialogue on longer-term positioning of UN Development System in the context of the 2030 Agenda for Sustainable Development* (Unpublished, 16 June 2016).
10 It is notable that this major change was implemented without amending the Charter, but rather through General Assembly resolution 60/251 of 15 March 2006.
11 General Assembly Resolution 64/289 adopted on 2 July 2010. See especially paragraph 49.
12 Puri, *Perilous Interventions*, 152.
13 GA resolution 71/3, 13 October 2016.
14 See, especially 69/321, 11 September 2015, op. 32–43 and 70/305, 13 September 2016, op. 34–45.

Suggested reading

There is an abundant bibliography about the United Nations which covers every facet imaginable, including the results of historical, analytical, thematic, and organizational research. The material covers books, articles, periodicals, and a vast trove of documents. No bibliography can do justice to the breadth and depth of this material. However, for any reader of this monograph who wishes to delve deeper into understanding the United Nations, the following sources are considered especially relevant.

Chesterman, Simon (ed.) *Secretary or General? The UN Secretary-General in World Politics* (Cambridge: Cambridge University Press, 2007).

Cooper, Andrew F., Jorge Heine, and Ramesh Thakur (eds) *The Oxford Handbook of Modern Diplomacy* (Oxford: Oxford University Press, 2013).

Lowe, Vaughan, Adam Roberts, Jennifer Welsh, and Dominik Zaum (eds) *The United Nations Security Council and War: The Evolution of Thought and Practice since 1945* (Oxford: Oxford University Press, 2010).

Luck, Edward C., *UN Security Council: Practice and Promise* (New York: Routledge, 2006).

Malone, David M., Sebastian von Einsiedel and Bruno Stagno Ugarte (eds) *The UN Security Council in the 21st Century* (Boulder, Col.: Lynne Rienner Publishes, 2016).

Peterson, M.J., *The United Nations General Assembly* (London: Routledge, 2005).

Schlesinger, Stephen C., *Act of Creation: The Founding of the United Nations* (Boulder, Col.: Westview Press, 2003).

Weiss, Thomas G. and Sam Daws (eds) *The Oxford Handbook on the United Nations* (Oxford: Oxford University Press, 2007).

Weiss, Thomas G., David P. Forsythe, Roger A. Coate, and Kelly-Kate Pease, *The United Nations and Changing World Politics* (Boulder, Col.: Westview, 2017), 8th edition.

Index